Who Put the Bomb
in Father Murphy's Chowder?

Other Books by Richard Frisbie

HOW TO PEEL A SOUR GRAPE

THE DO-IT-YOURSELF PARENT
(with Margery Frisbie)

Who Put the Bomb
in Father Murphy's Chowder?

IRREVERENT ESSAYS

•

By RICHARD FRISBIE

DOUBLEDAY & COMPANY, INC.
GARDEN CITY, NEW YORK
1968

Library of Congress Catalog Card Number 68–12772
Copyright © 1968 by Richard Frisbie
All Rights Reserved
Printed in the United States of America
First Edition

To my parents, Pearl and Os,
who always knew when *not* to laugh

ACKNOWLEDGMENTS

Some of the pieces in this book have appeared in magazines in somewhat different form. Their previous publication did not prevent me from revising them during the preparation of this book when I felt like it. Acknowledgment is made to the following magazines:

Extension—for "Please, Your Excellency, Don't Kiss the Baby," "How to Tell a Story with a Moral," "Let's Sit Some of Them Out," "Everyman Ecumenist (A Morality Play)," "Who Put the Bomb in Father Murphy's Chowder?", "WHERE Did You Say Two or Three Are Gathered Together?", "Remember to Keep Your Wedding Garment Handy," "Humbug, Humbug, Fly Away Home," "Is This On or Off the Record, Mr. Groundhog?", "Inside the Outside," "What Can You Expect from Slickers Who Wore Knickers?", and "Long May It Wave o'er the Land of the Careful."

U. S. Catholic—for "My Youth in the Middle Ages," "Is a Bassoon Twice as Holy as a Bass?", and "That's the Way the Martyr's Head Bounces."

The Sign—For "Richard Frisbie and His Giant Magnet."
Marriage—For "The Summer of My Discontent."
Catholic Press Annual—For "The Age of Renewals."

Contents

Who Put the Bomb
in Father Murphy's Chowder?

You'll Never Put Me on the Couch— I'll Move It First

A psychiatrist said the other day that in the future the only happy people will be those who are psychologically attuned to change as a way of life. I guess I'll be one of the happy ones. I like change.

It may be a bit unmanly to admit this, but I even like to rearrange furniture. Men are supposed to have fits when their wives move their favorite television chair as much as a foot to the right. You've probably seen this plot many times in situation comedy.

"Don't make any noise, Charlie, my wife's asleep."

"Shouldn't we turn on a light? I can't see a thing."

"Just follow me, Charlie. I know exactly where everything is. We're passing the coffee table now. Just keep to the right."

SOUND EFFECT: Crash.

Nothing like this could happen at our house. I'm the one who periodically begins to brood about the fact that the sofa has been in the same place for too long a time. It offends me, sitting there as if it were immortal. Mentally, I try it in different locations. My wife comes home from the store someday and finds all the living-room furniture stacked up in the dining room while I work out a more convenient new arrangement. One that, for example, will allow me to turn off the television, answer the phone, take a book from the bookshelves or close the door without getting up. (There must be some way.)

At least, that's how it used to be. I have to admit she finally rebelled and forbade further experiments. I am now allowed to rearrange only the furniture in my own study. This, however, does allow some scope for my talents. I keep making improvements in efficiency. Without moving from my chair, I can use the typewriter, the adding machine, the other telephone, the stapler, the hole puncher, the harmonica, the postal scale, the rubber cement, the tape recorder and the movie editor. I can reach stationery, envelopes, file folders, reference books, the window, the thermostat and the filing cabinet. Of course, I can get to the center of everything only on my hands and knees, but I am working on a new arrangement right now that should solve this problem.

In the past the world was basically conservative. New-fangled notions were accepted only after Galileo or somebody dropped a rock on the public's head.

"Now, Martha, if you'd take just *one* ride in Hiram's horseless carriage, you'd see for yourself how safe it really is. And if *we* had one, we could . . . why there goes Hiram now!"

SOUND EFFECT: Crash.

The average man today has learned to expect novelty in technology at least. Men in space, artificial hearts, lasers—yawn, yawn, where's the sports page? We're still conservative in some ways. The difference is that we are automatically progressive about some things, too, instead of always being conservative about everything. This creates some paradoxes.

Consider food. People will eat anything that is either cut in thin slices and salted or put in an aluminum tray and frozen, no matter how it tastes. When one cake package came out with a double lid, consumers thought the inner lid was frosting and ate it along with the food. It all tasted about the same. If anything, the lid was a little better. People like new packaging ideas. They're just waiting for the chance to spray scrambled eggs on their toast from an aerosol can.

But the ketchup industry has suffered heavy casualties among marketing vice presidents while failing to sell ketchup in a container that you can get the ketchup out of. Instead, consumers insist on the traditional narrow-necked bottle. It probably has something to do with an instinctive taboo against spilling blood. A thousand years from now when robots controlled by thought waves are doing all the work, your mechanical maid will come clanking in to serve the seaweedburgers with the same familiar ketchup bottle on the side.

Or shelter. With insulation, central heating, air conditioning, electrical outlets every six inches and automatic ice-cube makers, we live in comfort our ancestors could not imagine. But plumbing has made no progress in thousands of years. The ancient Cretans who put up the palace for King Minos knew enough to divert a small stream through the building to carry away wastes. We still solve the sanitation problem the same way—by flushing everything into the nearest creek. Actually, the Cretans were smarter; they didn't go snorkeling and water skiing in that same creek.

Leaving technology, we find similar inconsistencies in politics. As recently as 1918, Congress passed a Sedition Act providing that loudmouths could be sent to jail for "disloyal or abusive" language about the government. At this writing you can *say* anything you want about the government—as long as you don't burn your draft card. Why the authorities have had such a fixation about draft cards I don't know.

At the time of all the draft-card burnings I wondered why the demonstrators didn't burn their credit cards instead. From a distance, the cameramen wouldn't have known the difference. The demonstrators would have made their point without actually breaking the law and at the same time performed a public service. Destroying a credit card is always a public-spirited act, like planting a tree.

Even such a conservative force as religion has been rearranging its philosophical furniture since the Second Vatican Council. Despite all the changes, I haven't heard of a single person who has burned his Holy Name membership card to protest the new ways. At first people did seem a bit disturbed and uneasy when they went to mass on Sunday and found another change in the liturgy taking effect. Now they're going to the other extreme, complaining when there aren't any innovations.

"Why, this Sunday's mass was almost the same as last week's!"

"It only seems that way because Father gave the same sermon."

"No, I allowed for that. He always gives the same sermon."

One hears talk of further changes. Altars on wheels so they can be moved again if necessary. A new loose-leaf missal. An electric scoreboard for the front of the church from which directions on when to stand, sit and kneel can be flashed to the congregation via direct wire from Rome.

In the Catholic schools, parents used to enjoy only a circumscribed dialogue with teachers and administrators.

"We need a new roof for the school."

"How much will it cost?"

"Sixteen hundred and forty-eight dollars."

"We'll give a card party and raffle."

Public-school parents could express their interests in schools by going to P.T.A. meetings and listening to the principal give a speech on "the goals of education."

Nowadays Catholic parents can go to home-school meetings to hear a speech on "the goals of education" and continue an enriched form of dialogue with teachers, administrators and members of the lay school board.

"We need a new roof for the school."

"How much will it cost?"

"Thirty-two hundred and ninety-six dollars."

"We'll have to give TWO card parties."

In higher education, the new spirit of change expresses itself in self-study programs. A team of outside experts studies the college and tells the faculty what's wrong with the school. Then the faculty holds its own meetings to extend the list. The outsiders didn't know the half of it. In the old days, the students had to perform this critical function all by themselves. And no one filed the minutes of THEIR discussions in the president's office.

The winds of change are rustling the Protestants, too.

Merger talks began in 1966 among eight denominations with twenty-four million members. The discussions are expected to continue for several years. Protestants let everyone have his say, and if each of the twenty-four million took one turn, the discussions would last two or three thousand years. Fortunately, our national habit of everybody talking at once can be expected to speed things up.

At issue are such basic matters as whether worship should be liturgical or plain and whether bishops are necessary. Not too many years ago men were likely to come to blows over such questions instead of discussing them amicably. If we Catholics had caught them in such a discussion—amicable or otherwise—we'd have burned the lot at the stake. Now we invite them to ecumenical dinners, at which the most pressing problem is remembering which denominations don't hold with alcoholic beverages.

New trends are stirring in the basic unit of society, the family. There is a shift in emphasis from reproduction toward companionship and self-fulfillment. In the face of the population problem, the contraception controversy seems likely to be resolved by technology as much as by theology. We hear more and more about interpersonal relationships and group dynamics.

The logical outcome of all this is a basic marriage unit, not of one man and one woman, but of five persons. Five has been found the best number for interaction in group-dynamics experiments. Two is outmoded. Three would be a triangle, and the whole of history and literature proves what a mistake that would be. Four, consisting of two couples, would encourage the development of factions in the family and lead to unresolvable differences of opinion. More than five would be too many for such an intimate bond.

But five—three men and two women or vice versa—would be just right. Family decisions by majority vote would be easily reached. Scarcely anyone would be widowed or orphaned till late in life. There'd always be somebody home to watch the children, and it would be hard to decide who's to blame for not writing the amount of the check on the stub in the check-book. This new kind of family ought to get along better.

I can foresee some problems. Courtship would become complicated with five persons trying to arrange dates between bowling nights. The wedding would require a fantastic amount of champagne with five parents for each participant. That's twenty-five brides' and grooms' mothers and fathers, up to one hundred twenty-five grandparents and countless brothers, sisters, aunts, uncles and cousins—all standing around thirsty.

The New Family would have to give up some things. "His" and "hers" towels. Tea for two. Sports cars with bucket seats. But they'd certainly have community.

One must keep an open mind about the new possibilities in this era of change. A friend of mine accidentally put a St. Christopher medal in a parking meter the other day. The meter rang up three bell-fruits and paid a jackpot of $18.13. Once this would have been regarded as a miracle, but we are finally rooting superstition and belief in magic out of our religion. Instead of building a shrine on the spot, my friend merely threw the thirteen pennies over his left shoulder at exactly midnight and went off to spend the $18.00.

While we're getting rid of magic, perhaps we can shed stuffiness also. Despite the example of such saints as Francis of Assisi, Philip Neri, Thomas More and innumerable others, the pious have shown a distressing tendency over the centuries to be less charming than the rascals.

I recently translated an old Latin manuscript telling of the rivalry between one Sententius, the chief of the wool merchants' guild, and a low character called Reynard the Cutpurse. Sententius endowed nine convents and was trusted by everyone, but for an evening of chatter and laughter the most popular man in town was Reynard. The people of the town even coined a proverb, "amo, amas, amat, amamus, amatis, amant," which means "If you hide the silver before he comes, that Reynard is lots of laughs." Nobody made up any sayings about poor Sententius.

In the days when the king was really the boss, society found a way around the limits of one man's personality by providing the institution of the court jester. When the king was entertaining some of his more grandiose notions, the jester at least had a chance to try to head him off by dropping a few wisecracks.

Something similar could be tried in the councils of the churches. Every diocese, religious order, presbytery, council of deacons, lay organization or whatever could have an extra secretary selected for his inability to keep a straight face at moments of crisis.

"And what are you laughing at now, Father?"

"I'm sorry, Your Excellency, it's just—ha, ha, ha—just that this letter of yours about what time nuns have to go to bed—ho, ho, ho—seems a bit much."

"You think it might give scandal?"

"Well, suppose the cartoonists do a bit on it in the funnies. They'll exaggerate it terribly. They'll have this nun who's president of a college and a famous scholar. The President of the United States will be trying to get her on the phone to ask her advice about an emergency, but it's past ten o'clock local time and nobody answers because the curfew made them all go to bed."

"Well, she can have a phone in her room, can't she?"

"Your Excellency forgets the paragraph about honoring the spirit as well as the letter of the law. At ten o'clock all the phones and electricity are automatically disconnected and—ho, ho, ho—steel shutters drop down over the windows and doors. Maybe they'll do a skit about it on television, too."

SOUND EFFECT: Letter being torn up.

Or—

"Why are you looking at me like that Helen?"

"It's this resolution, Dorothy—tee, hee, hee—forgive me. I see we're—ha, ha—going after dirty books again."

"You don't think we should?"

"Did anyone on the board read any of the books?"

"I should say not!"

"Well, I've been looking at the list and I think I ought to tell you—snicker, snicker—that *Myrtle Behind the House, Rosemary in the Flower Bed* is a GARDENING book."

"Oh."

As I said, I think I'll be one of the happy ones. I'll be able to adjust to the changes as they come. Even if things should go as far as the five-spouses-in-a-family plan in my lifetime, I'll know exactly what to do. I'll pick up two votes for a majority and try the sofa on the other side of the living room with the brown chairs shoved together under the lamp.

Be Kind to Your Cellmate—
She May Be Somebody's Mother Superior

When I was a beginning police reporter, the city editor always demanded that I check to see whether the protagonist in any remotely newsworthy arrest had a police record. The files of the police department were regarded as everyman's *Who's Who*. Or, more correctly, *Who's Nobody*.

A man with a record was obviously tough and no good, unless the record was for public drunkenness, which meant the subject was merely weak and no good. In either case, his photograph with the little number under his chin was scarcely a passport to the society page.

A newspaper needs biographical information in order to interpret the bare facts. Suppose the police apprehend a man walking around in a bookstore with a flashlight at three o'clock in the morning. If he has an arrest record, the editors immediately recognize the story, a widely anthologized classic:

COPS NAB EX-CON IN BOOKSTORE BURGLARY

But suppose the prowler has no record. This complicates matters and, as a practical matter, makes a libel suit more difficult to defend if it should come to that. The editors can't be sure whether they are confronted with a comedy:

TIPSY BOOKKEEPER TRIES
TO BALANCE WRONG BOOKS

Or a tragedy:

FATHER OF 7 CAUGHT
BREAKING INTO BOOKSTORE

I suppose reporters still check on such matters, newspaper tradition being what it is, but a police record doesn't mean what it used to. Now all the best people are rapidly acquiring them through the civil rights movement.

Priests, society matrons, rabbis, theatrical celebrities, nuns, congressmen's wives and sons, ministers, governor's mothers— all the people you might expect to meet in the dining room of a stuffy convention hotel are turning up instead in the clink. If this sort of thing keeps up, the day may come when it will be considered more dignified to ride in the paddy wagon than in a limousine with a chauffeur.

Let us imagine a scene a few years from now when certain chancery officials are considering various candidates for the pastorate of a key parish. One man speaks:

"You will recall, Your Excellency, that at our last meeting we narrowed down the field to three men. Now I have collected the additional information about them you asked for."

"Ah, yes," the bishop nods. "You have the police records?"

"Precisely. And excellent ones they are. Here's Father Brown's record—fourteen arrests, three convictions and fines totaling $300."

Several monsignors murmur approvingly. A second file is opened.

"And listen to this—Father Jones has been arrested twenty-seven times, with nine convictions. Montgomery, Birmingham, Selma, Rochester, Chicago. All the best places."

"That's inspiring," says the bishop. "The convictions—what were the charges?"

"All the usual ones. Parading without a permit, disturbing the peace, inciting to riot, blocking traffic, harboring a runaway slave, failure to salute the Confederate flag. Also, resisting arrest and assaulting a policeman."

The bishop frowns. "Perhaps Father Jones is a bit over-zealous."

"I know him, Your Excellency. He could use a little more experience and seasoning. On the other hand, that parish out there is as square as they come. They need a swinger like Father Jones to shake them up."

The bishop points to the third file. "What about Father Smith?"

"Nothing here but two parking tickets and a $10 fine for driving the wrong way on a one-way street."

"He might at least have gone through a red light," one of the monsignors mutters.

"No sense of commitment," says another monsignor. "And him a seminary professor."

"Don't worry about the seminary," the bishop comments. "Fine bunch of men. Most of them have done a stretch up the river, and the rector is out on parole right now."

Chancery offices are not the only places where a police record may be honored in the future. College registrars may begin to balance a "C" in high school chemistry against thirty days in the right jail for the right reason. Politicians will have to update their tactics. Eventually, some senator will get up to make a speech waving a file folder at the press gallery. "I have right here in my hands a list of the names of sixty-seven highly placed government officials who have never—I repeat, never—

spent a single day in the custody of any law enforcement agency within the boundaries of these United States."

The strict fundamentalist denominations that require members to tithe a literal ten per cent of their incomes may start giving credit for bail bond receipts.

Perhaps courses on approved passive resistance techniques will be introduced into seminaries and novitiates. From there they can spread to business schools, like the University of Chicago and Harvard, which like to encourage the altruistic and statesmanlike approach to business.

Ultimately, we'll see a new kind of organization man working his way up in the big corporations. Bright young men will make themselves noticed by chaining themselves to the boss's aspirin bottle to protest anti-social directives. This kind of enthusiasm and enterprise, plus a proper background in Ivy League jails, can mark future leaders for advancement.

But where does this leave a man with an old-fashioned police record for mere felony? No longer will he be able to cow the rest of the customers at the bar by announcing, "I got a record." Instead of edging away to avoid trouble, the customers will think he's leading up to a civil rights story. Assuming he's taking up a collection to bail some nuns out of the pokey, they'll pass the hat.

My Youth in the Middle Ages

When the time comes for feeling middle-aged, Catholics are MORE middle-aged than anyone else. This is because only a Catholic can be old enough to have spent his youth in the Middle Ages.

I, for example, attended the *schola* attached to a huge Gothic church, where students were taught that the thirteenth was the greatest of centuries. We were all quite ready to believe that what was good enough for the thirteenth century was good enough for us. I say this without apology. None of my neighbors lived in the twentieth century. The Protestants mostly lived in the sixteenth century, which, as simple arithmetic proves, was closer to the thirteenth century than to the twentieth.

There was a man on my block whose calendar had stopped several thousand years B.C. He had a rock garden—a sort of miniature Stonehenge—where he worked off the after-effects of sundown rites at a primitive temple known as Clancy's. He chased us with a club whenever we tried a short cut through the sacred stones. Obviously, a purely paleolithic type.

Surrounded by so many variations in the time scale, we Catholics might have been tempted to forget occasionally that our century was the thirteenth. To protect us from confusion on this point, we had several aids. One was the diocesan newspaper, whose existence was rather a mystery since Gutenberg hadn't yet invented movable type.

Our diocesan editor apparently believed the secular news media were engaged in a gigantic conspiracy to tell lies about the Catholic Church. He had expressed his theory in a formula: the specific gravity of the presumed lie equals the degree of implied criticism of things Catholic—squared.

If some minor battle of the Spanish Civil War resulted in a setback for the Franco forces, all papers reporting this news became automatically suspect. Any secular correspondent who suggested that local politicians in Catholic regions of Europe or South America ought to take more interest in social reform was assumed to be a fellow-traveler—unless he based his comments on quotations from Pope Leo XIII or Pope Pius XI, which made it all right (at least in our diocese).

History books give the year 1291 as the end of the Crusades. Possibly history books are part of the conspiracy. One crusade was still in progress when I was in school. Our teacher told us about the cosmic struggle between the Catholics and the Others. She kept careful score and brought us up to date every few days.

Hollywood fan magazines would reveal that a prominent movie actress was a convert to Catholicism. Score one for our side. A Catholic lecturer would refute those embarrassing stories about the Spanish Inquisition and the Galileo case, all in one breath. Score another one for our side. Then the same actress would sue her husband for divorce. Oops, a point for Them, narrowing our lead at the end of the quarter. If it happened to be a good year, Notre Dame would clobber Southern Methodist about Thanksgiving time, and we'd finish the semester well out ahead.

In those long-ago days, religion displayed a breach-the-barbican competitiveness which the gentle ecumenical spirit of Vatican II lately has laid to rest. Among laymen it used to take the form of pamphlet passing. The typical Pamphlet Passer believed himself surrounded either by panting potential converts or the paynim enemy.

If a non-Catholic neighbor asked two or three questions about the Church out of mild curiosity, a Pamphlet Passer would impale him with one of the tracts he carried on his person at all times. The victim probably would be too polite to hand it back, so later the Pamphlet Passer would confide to you that so-and-so was just about "ready."

The Pamphlet Passer must not be confused with the genuinely apostolic layman who, then as now, actually did bring questioning souls into the Church. The difference was in motive. A rampant Pamphlet Passer was competing against the Others. His pamphlets were his approximation of a Notre Dame forward pass or a thirteenth-century mace banging the Saracen infidels on the head.

Many of the pamphlets he used would not be tolerated today on the church-door racks of even the more conservative and changeless parishes. Over the centuries, the mind of the Church has emphasized different truths at different times. Considering the variation in outlook between such Fathers of the Church as Augustine and Aquinas, we should not be scandalized to recall that obscure clerics writing for obscure presses sometimes recommended brands of spirituality scarcely recognizable to the Church of *aggiornamento*.

An example that sticks in my mind, even after all the intervening centuries, is one church-door pamphlet devoted to the pastor's favorite novena. The pamphlet just missed making the novena an eighth sacrament. As for the novena service itself, the most striking feature was the remarkable way it isolated participants from the time sense of the workaday world.

Week after week they sang, "Good Night, Sweet Jesus," at nine o'clock in the morning and never seemed to think it the least bit incongruous.

One of my friends took to reading pamphlets of the inferior sort after the novena. Without any of us noticing at first, he gradually became addicted to pamphlet-rack piety. I finally suspected what was happening to him when I saw bruises on his forehead.

Upon being accused, he broke down and admitted that he had been self-levitating. That's how he had bruised his head. In the actual thirteenth century, doorways had pointed Gothic arches, and a self-levitator could float right through, as long as he wasn't more than a couple of feet off the ground. But on the low transoms of modern doorways my friend kept bumping his head.

With considerable effort, I persuaded him to consult a wise priest who is especially good at dealing with difficult cases. The last time I saw my friend, Father had worked him up to 1870 and was optimistic that his progress would continue.

Please, Your Excellency, Don't Kiss the Baby

Time was when the bishop was merely *there*—a presence like the cathedral itself or the force of gravity. People took him for granted. Now, for better or for worse, his every word and deed are scrutinized, analyzed and psychoanalyzed. He can't even say, "No comment," without some people accusing him of taking the wrong stand and others wondering what he meant by a smart remark like that.

This is not the first time in the long history of the Church that the role of the bishops has changed. The question isn't particularly theological. It's more a matter of sociology, psychology, political science and the kind of leadership that moved the people of a given era.

The earliest bishops, from the point of view of polite Roman society, were a passel of hippies. Bearded, dusty-robed, unwashed, they stood on soap boxes and preached in the market place. Or, if a persecution happened to be going on, they and their followers held secret underground gatherings like Communists plotting to overthrow the government.

In medieval times, the bishop was an entirely different type of man. He was likely to be the younger brother of a secular lord. He himself often had received the same knightly upbringing as the warlike nobility. Before he began devoting his attention to his career in the Church, he might very well have been more skillful with sword and lance than his older brother, the Duke.

For instance, generally overlooked amid the attention given traditional Christian martyrs such as Thomas à Becket is the story of the good Bishop Otto of Liverwurst. His brother, the Duke of Liverwurst, ran a protection racket. For regular monthly payments, the Duke and his men would protect the merchants of Liverwurst from such risks as being strung up by the thumbs over a slow fire. Since the Duke was the only person in the region who hung merchants by their thumbs over slow fires, his clients could count on being left in peace as long as they paid up.

Kindly Bishop Otto did not approve. As a man of his times, he didn't see anything wrong with cuffing the serfs around a little, but he drew the line at torture and extortion. He protested to his brother time after time.

Finally, the Duke, tired of Otto's incessant interference, sent four of his most trusted henchmen to murder Otto while he was saying mass in the cathedral. This was a mistake. Otto, who had been singularly athletic in his youth, parried their swords with his crozier and brained all four of them with the heavy brass base of a candlestick. Then, understandably incensed, he rallied a band of sturdy clerics and yeomen, who marched on the castle, threw the guards into the moat, and seized the Duke.

When the Duke had been bricked up in a wall for about a week, he saw the error of his ways and repented. Otto might have been revered to this day in Liverwurst—canonization in earlier times could occur by acclamation—but for a certain rigidity of character. The fact that he never let the Duke out of the wall cast a shadow over his image.

During the Renaissance, the bishops of the smaller dioceses were free to take an interest in charitable foundations and various spiritual matters, but the big time bishops in the public eye had to be art patrons and diplomats, especially the latter. The public might forgive them a lapse of taste, but to fumble in the game of playing off the king against his powerful relatives was unthinkable.

In my private museum I have a seminary catalogue from the fifteenth century listing special courses for advanced students in codes, invisible inks, espionage and document forging (supported, of course, by a secret grant from the CIA).

In our times, people don't think much of the kinds of leaders they used to look up to. A king ranks somewhat lower than a baseball player or a folk singer. Military heroes command only slight influence because there are too many ex-dogfaces around who know who really won the battles. The diplomats, who seem unable to settle any ruction bigger than a softball game, are never asked for autographs.

Unfortunately, secular styles in leadership affect the roles of bishops. The barefoot bishops conquered the Roman Empire in their day, but since the Industrial Revolution created the businessman-hero it has been difficult to imagine a beatnik bishop mixing easily with government and business officials or addressing a communion breakfast.

Many commentators have compared American bishops with businessmen. "Administrators," "fund-raisers," "brick-layers" and similar terms have been hurled at bishops like eggs and tomatoes. This isn't fair. If bishops of the recent past hadn't been somewhat competent in property management, the faithful would be sitting out in the rain whenever they gathered in greater numbers than would fit into a living room. What's more, Americans wanted their bishop to resemble the boss at work. It made them feel at home every day of the week.

Suddenly, the businessman seems no longer the masterful father figure who guided and protected us when our civilization was awkward and immature. Those businessmen who haven't been sent to jail for price fixing have been replaced by decision-making computers. At the same time, the bishops are extending the principle of collegiality into their own dioceses by setting up parish and diocesan councils. The trend toward democratizing the Church clearly is growing stronger.

The bishops of the future, instead of being prince-bishops, or diplomat-bishops or administrator-bishops, may have to be politician-bishops. Will there be direct popular elections, with parties and torchlight parades and campaign promises?

"I promise that if I am elected your bishop, this diocese will enjoy the lowest per capita expenses of any diocese in the country."

Or:

"Elect me your bishop and we'll get this place moving again —new churches, new schools, something for everybody."

We can hope the pendulum won't swing that far. However, the new structure of the Church will require considerable skill in the art of politics, from all concerned. The Italians will be lobbying for St. Joseph's Day to be given as much attention as St. Patrick's Day. There'll be vote swapping in the diocesan council, with the lay delegates supporting longer vacations for priests in return for a few more committee chairmanships. Women will be lobbying for equal-rights legislation, which may lead to a filibuster in the diocesan senate.

It's not inconceivable that we'll find ourselves nostalgic for the firm hand of the good Bishop Otto.

A Band of Barefoot Angels Comin' after Me

Catholics of my generation grew up with strange images, if not strange gods. I once heard a distinguished theologian confess that despite his lifelong studies (and he was a widely respected scholar) he never had been able to shake off entirely his childhood image of his soul as a big white football inside his chest.

This may show how theological scholars have a natural aptitude for their work. My own childhood image of the soul was much less definite. I thought of it, rather nebulously, as an expanse of white fabric of indefinite size, somewhere between a bath towel and a bedsheet.

For years I sat on the left half of my seat in school in order not to push my guardian angel onto the floor. Most of the other children in the school did the same. This was a remarkable survival, considering that St. Thomas Aquinas, who insisted strongly that angels are not merely invisible people, was canonized as long ago as 1323.

Progress is more elusive than one might think. I can name at least one child who, even today, has been told that a guardian angel sits on his right shoulder telling him to be good and not listen to the devil sitting on his left shoulder. In my youth, the unseen spirits only sat *with* you, not *on* you.

The partly reformed liturgy is still a rich source of untheological and distracting images, even for adults. At this writing, an offertory hymn frequently in use in my parish includes the following lines:

> May our souls be pure and spotless
> As the host of wheat so fine;
> May all stain of sin be crushed out,
> Like the grape that forms the wine.

Just before this is sung by the congregation, we recite the genuine poetry of the Psalms, which has inspired piety in men's hearts since Old Testament times. But as soon as we start singing about the squashed grape, the inspired moment passes. The untheological image I see is that of my soul being trampled in a big wooden vat by a crowd of barefoot angels (presumably the ones who couldn't find seats in today's overcrowded classrooms).

The Church needs new images to help make religion meaningful in contemporary terms, but paradoxically it is recent material that creates the image problems. Most Biblical imagery is still forceful and pertinent.

The Prodigal Son is still among us. I knew him in college. The last I heard, he was separated from his wife and out of work, his attempt to grow red, white and blue striped bacon on his experimental pig farm having failed. His friends are hoping he'll find the way home some day.

Good Samaritans are in sufficient supply to appear in the newspapers every few weeks. Now, as *then*, their deeds are just uncommon enough to make news.

Even in an urbanized society, the Good Shepherd is a clear enough image. One does not have to be a fleece-carrying Merino to grasp its significance.

The wise and foolish virgins may seem a bit strange in our culture (what business does a bridegroom have at midnight with ten young girls?), but a moment's thought, aided perhaps by a footnote, makes the meaning of the symbolism sufficiently clear to be useful.

I was thinking over this problem of images one night while

sitting in my car in front of a store where my wife was shopping.
A light rain was beginning to fall. Suddenly the car door opened,
and a man slid in beside me. Startled, I sputtered objections.

"Shut up," he said. "I'm your guardian angel."

I recognized the voice of a jocular and outspoken fellow parishioner, Ignatius Aloysius Murphy, with whom it was easy to
fall into a discussion of improving the Church. It is his favorite
subject.

On this occasion I brought up the Church's need to improve
some of its images, or at least to discard some of the irrelevant
ones. I suggested that perhaps professional image-makers could
help.

Murphy said that idea was so old he first heard it on the
way home from one of the Crusades (after so many years
he couldn't remember whether it was the Second or the Third).

I persisted, arguing that in the past the Church has known
how to put image-makers to good use. St. Paul, with his circulating letters and market-center preaching, was an expert with
mass media of the first century. Gothic architecture was invented between 1137 and 1144 just outside Paris and spread
immediately throughout Europe. The great works of Renaissance art that have become part of religious tradition were
mostly bought from popular commercial artists and paid for at
the going rate.

Murphy saw the point at once. "We could lay out the cash
to employ professional composers and maybe even a theatrical
director to work on the liturgy."

I said I supposed many of the faithful would be shocked at
the thought of commercial image-makers being paid to meddle
in something as sacred as worship.

"Latent Puritanism," Murphy snorted. "It wouldn't have to
be Hollywood taste, unauthorized texts or anything heretical."

It did seem to me, I said, that professionals could be assigned
to work within particular limits and do a good job because
they know how. However, I was troubled by the problem of

getting approvals. Is it really conceivable that a task force of show-biz or ad people, no matter how worthy their private lives or their efforts, could obtain the support of the Church?

Murphy thought so. "The professionals are used to dealing every day with Broadway producers and clients and television network executives. Say what you will about the Church, no chancery office is any worse."

The rain had stopped. Leaving me with this thought, Murphy spread his golden wings and flew away.

Is a Bassoon Twice as Holy as a Bass?

I always wonder if there's something wrong with our approach to liturgical music when I hear singing at mass on Sunday morning that's less tuneful than the singing the night before at the Bit 'o Erin Tap, and a good deal less spirited. Any doubt is dispelled when the news reaches me of controversies about whether the guitar is an instrument suitable for use in church.

Opinion seems to split according to age. Young folks (who have yet to distinguish themselves at the collection basket) are eager to picket and carry signs in favor of guitars. Elderly bishops and pastors are inclined to banish them, root, branch and pick.

The resulting need to compute the relative holiness of various instruments creates a whole new department of musicology. Obviously, an organ is holier than a guitar. With some of the other instruments, calculating the Relative Holiness Quotient is more difficult. For the benefit of those who wish to pursue the subject, I offer the following preliminary observations. They are certain to be revised, once scholars have had the opportunity to study the field as deeply as it deserves.

In general, the R.H.Q. (Relative Holiness Quotient) varies in proportion to the square of the instrument's distance from a Hootenanny. The viola, therefore, is the holiest instrument of the string ensemble, followed closely by the cello. The violin may be tolerated under some circumstances, but the bass viol, being the mainstay of so many popular combos, has an R.H.Q. of zero, along with mandolins, ukeleles, balalaikas and samisens (except in Nagasaki, where a special dispensation may have remained in effect since the days of the sixteenth-century martyrs).

As is well known to students of popular religious symbolism, the harp is in a special category of its own.

Among the brasses, the trumpet has impeccable credentials, being the favorite instrument of a number of angels, even when on official business. On doctrinal grounds, there would be no objection to the tuba, which, having been invented by Tubalcain, has Scriptural antecedants also; or to the euphonium (named for St. Euphonius); or to the sousaphone, which, like the pretzel, contains a certain religious symbolism in its very form. However, the demand for these three instruments by composers of liturgical music continues light. No other brasses are at all acceptable. Cornets and trombones suffer from long association with Dixieland jazz, which was basically Protestant, and Fundamentalist at that. The French horn is tainted both by its vulgar descent from hunting horns and its association with the Gallican party in their disputes with the Ultramontanists.

In the wood-wind choir, the villain is the saxophone, which may not even be buried in consecrated ground. The clarinet (Benny Goodman and Artie Shaw notwithstanding), flute, piccolo, oboe and bassoon are all innocuous enough. The once-faithful English horn was excommunicated along with Henry VIII in the sixteenth century.

Use of percussion in liturgical music has a Scriptural basis, since the Old Testament speaks in numerous passages of praising the Lord with the sound of the timbrel. This instrument was a kind of tambourine. Since the Biblical authorization is quite clear, it is rather strange that one never hears liturgical music written for mixed voices and tambourines. Whether such other percussion instruments as snare and bass drums and timpani can be classified loosely as varieties of tambourine is a matter for further discussion by the scholars. One may safely assume they would rule out such excesses as wood blocks, temple gongs and snare drums played with brushes.

Marimbas and bongo drums, if played within a quarter mile of a church, must be exorcised.

There are many practical reasons for retaining the organ as the basic instrument for church music. If the congregation should choose to sing out on occasion, no other instrument has the massive strength required to keep them more or less on key. And to match the varied tone color of the organ's different voices with other instruments, the pastor would have to hire a whole orchestra instead of a single organist. Since many organs won't be paid for until many more years of *aggiornamento* have passed, keeping the organ as the standard by which the R.H.Q. of other instruments is measured is an economic necessity.

Some scholars believe the R.H.Q. computations would be more accurate if a greater number of parishes were willing to hire organists who know that an organ is an organ and not a big piano with a lot of extra pedals.

It will be a pity if further research on the early Church puts the organ under a cloud. Unfortunately, there are indications that the first organs had strong secular associations. Cicero, for instance, speaks of the delight of hearing organ music at banquets. And everyone knows what Roman banquets were like in those days! A good Holy Name man would have felt uncomfortable, to say the least.

Some commentators go so far as to say that the organ never would have been accepted in the Church but for the work that pumping the bellows made for idle hands. Even today, when bellows-pumping has been eliminated by technology, an organ keeps the organist's hands *and feet* fully occupied.

That's an advantage that can be claimed for few other instruments.

After the foregoing observations had been published in several magazines, including the Philippine *Catholic Digest*, I received a letter pointing out that there is a traditional mass in the Philippines that requires not only tambourines but castanets as well. According to the Reverend Joseph I. Stoffel, S.J., of Malaybalay, Bukidnon, Philippines, the *Misa Pastoril* ("Shepherds' Mass") has been sung for at least fifty years at the daily predawn high mass during the nine days preceding Christmas. The custom may go back for centuries.

Father Stoffel wrote:

I can't testify that the tambourines and castanets are written in the score (being musically illiterate I can't read the score) but they must be there. I have heard this mass many, many times, and never without tambourines and castanets. All the older parishes, especially where the pastor is ultra-conservative, have sets of tambourines and castanets for the purpose, in the choir loft music cabinet. It is inconceivable that a bishop would forbid them. Men as rash as that just don't become bishops.

The music of this mass is gay and lively, like Spanish dance music. I suppose it is of Andalusian origin. The first time I heard it was a startling experience, but by the time mass was ended I would not have been surprised if the organ had played "La Paloma" for the recessional.

In one old, tradition-bound parish, resistant to modern innovations, where I was the pastor some years back, we had all those instruments plus a full brass band for the pre-Christmas masses. There was a special place in the choir loft for the band.

Upon reading this letter, I became excited at the thought of brass bands in the choir lofts in this country. When a bishop visits a parish, he could hear "Hail to the Chief" instead of "Ecce Sacerdos Magnus." Or, if there was a great gathering of bishops, they could march in procession while the band played "The Stars and Stripes Forever" in recognition of the lack of episcopal opposition to the government on the Vietnam question.

How to Tell a Story with a Moral

They don't tell pointed stories as well as they used to. Aesop's greedy dog grabbed for the reflected bone and dropped his real one in the creek. Any dolt could tell it served the dog right. Beatrix Potter's Peter Rabbit disobeyed his mother, brought misfortune upon himself and presumably learned a lesson. Simple, clear, realistic. The art seems to have been lost.

The pointed story too easily becomes pious. At the grammar school level there's the story about St. Peter Lepus, the boy saint. As a small boy, Peter fell into the habit of using bad language. Being basically a good boy, he agreed to cooperate with a plan suggested by his mother. Every time he said a bad word, he went out into the backyard and hammered a nail in the wall of the garage.

In a short time—alas for Peter's good intentions—the garage was studded with nailheads. Since Peter was unskilled with the hammer, he kept hitting his thumb, saying another bad word and having to drive another nail.

Peter wearied of having sore thumbs all the time. He gradually conquered his bad habit. Whenever a day passed without a single bad word, he went to the garage and pulled out a nail. I'm sorry I can't tell you exactly what the moral of this story is supposed to be. When I heard it, I became distracted waiting for the garage to fall down.

A story I remember in more detail from my youth was a favorite among retreat masters who specialized in boys' high schools. It was about another boy named Peter, who early displayed a disregard for morality in a notorious escapade at Mac-Gregor's Drive In.

As Peter grew older, he took to hanging around with an undesirable element despite the repeated warnings of his good mother. One night, with a pack of his hoodlum friends, he robbed a saloon called The Lettuce Patch and shot the bartender. Later the same night, while spending his share of the loot in a night club with Floozie Cottontail, Peter was rubbed out in his tracks—unshriven—by Wolfgang the Eraser.

The retreatants were expected to conclude that if they sinned, they, too, might be snatched off to Hell before they could repent.

Nowadays, the story with a moral is likely to contain more sociology than fire and brimstone. Here's one that could be sung to guitar accompaniment by young sisters and clerics.

Peter was a black rabbit who wanted to move his family to Burrowton, where the white rabbits lived on the other side of Mr. MacGregor's gooseberry patch. When the white rabbits found out, they blinked their pink eyes and complained they might lose their life savings, which were invested in their burrows. At first, they aroused some public sympathy for their point of view. Then an impartial investigation headed by Senator MacGregor exposed the white rabbit argument as a fallacy.

The MacGregor Committee proved the savings represented by burrow ownership to be an illusion at all stages of the mortgage. After five years, the owner's monthly payments still go mostly for interest, and his equity in the property could be concealed easily behind a radish. After ten years, the owner's equity just about balances the depreciation at two per cent a year. He soon needs a new roof and other items that cost him plenty in time, money and worry. After twenty or thirty years, the owner receives clear title to the burrow, but if he thinks of his title as an asset, he's wrong.

In theory, burrow ownership is cheaper in the long run than renting because the owner does the maintenance work in his spare time instead of paying a professional to do it. Actually, when the average burrow-owner begins a do-it-yourself project, the odds are 9.3 to 1 (MacGregor Committee statistics) that he'll botch it and end up depreciating the property. By the time the burrow has been paid for, it has been subjected to a generation of do-it-yourself maintenance and remodeling. Regardless of what Peter the black rabbit does, the white rabbit burrows clearly are more liability than asset.

Since the modern trend in moral stories reflects our times, this one is non-directive. You have to write your own ending. A few packaged endings are furnished herewith only as a convenience for readers:

1. Liberal white rabbits organize an open-burrow movement. Peter and his family move in, and everyone lives happily ever after.

2. When Peter and his wife inspect the burrows on the market, they decide they wouldn't live in one of those shacks if you gave it to them. Instead, they bypass crumbling Burrowton entirely to settle in Gooseberry Vista, a brand-new subdivision with FHA financing open to all.

3. The State Highway Department chooses Burrowton as the best place for a new throughway cloverleaf. Burrowton ceases to exist.

One can detect echoes of the moral tale in contemporary literature like the new play from the Theater of the Absurd, *The Rabbit*.

In the first act, a middle-aged man goes to the refrigerator in his bachelor apartment to get out a bunch of carrots. He counts the carrots over and over, coming out with a different number every time. The elderly woman who owns the apartment building enters. He accuses her of stealing some of his carrots. Her reply is ambiguous. In a rage, he thumps her with his hind foot and throws her out. Counting his carrots again, he finds he now has more than before.

In the second act, two policemen appear, investigating the murder of the landlady, whose body has been found on the stairs. The man, on learning his visitors are policemen, thinks they have come to solve his problem of recurrent carrot thefts. He mentions several persons in the neighborhood as likely suspects. The policemen, who think he is talking about the murder, take copious notes. As the scene progresses, it gradually becomes obvious that the man is turning into a rabbit. He finally hops away, lippety-lippety.

The third act reveals for the first time the policemen's names, Foxx and MacGregor. They seem to have moved into the rabbit's apartment; at least, they are cooking something and making elaborate preparations for an unnamed guest who is expected momentarily. Their cooking continues, and the audience learns that the main dish is to be rabbit stew. Finally, the doorbell rings. The landlady enters, carrying a bunch of carrots. Curtain.

Critics have interpreted this play variously. For some, it is a statement of protest against modern materialism, with carrots (karats!) used as a symbol of wealth. Others see it as a play about fear, in which the central character's paranoid suspicions multiply (like rabbits) until he becomes not only a scared rabbit but a stewed one as well. A few critics stress the theme of love, symbolized by the landlady who keeps bringing carrots no matter what.

This apparently was the interpretation favored by the producers of the film version, *The Sound of Rabbits*. In the movie, the landlady is younger and marries the man in the apartment. Baron Peter von Hasenpfeffer. The movie ends when she begins a concert tour with the Baron and all the little Hasenpfeffers, whom she has taught to dance, sing and play the sweet potato.

The story with a moral has become very big at the box office —as long as no one can tell for sure what it is.

Let's Sit Some of Them Out

Researchers at the University of Pittsburgh's School of Medicine have discovered that the human body instinctively "dances" to the rhythm of speech. People can't help making subtle movements of fingers, toes, eyebrows and other appendages to mark the beat of what we're saying. Mediterranean peoples are famous for being unable to talk without waving their hands. Even the most phlegmatic of us, apparently, obeys the same impulse on a less dramatic scale.

This discovery suggests a new way to analyze some of the words and phrases currently being more widely used than understood. An abstract idea becomes easier to grasp when you can associate it with a concrete image. So I think some of the more troublesome words should be choreographed rather than defined.

Consider "credibility," for example. This is a masked ball, at which impenetrably disguised partners whirl to the music until seconds before midnight. Then, just before the bomb goes off, the masks are dropped and we see that the Cowboy wasn't dancing with the Princess, as everyone thought, but with a low-bred wench, who sneaked in from the scullery.

And no one can afford to miss the Dance of the Doves and Hawks. The Doves pretend the Hawks are vultures, and the Hawks pretend the Doves are chicken. While all this poultry is flapping around, Mother Goose is hatching a new set of problems.

One of them is "alienation," which obviously is a solo. Another is "identity crisis," reviewed by one dance critic as "the Big Apple—with a worm in it." Still another is "depersonalization," in which one dancer lies down and all the others trample him.

Many areas of human activity are teeming with words that demand kinetic interpretation. In the arts, "I know what I like" is a square dance, i.e., a dance for squares. "Contemporary," with its search for impact and emphasis on the exotic, has to be performed by one of those touring groups of native girls who dance bare-breasted in the more cosmopolitan cities where the police let them.

"Contemporary" is not to be confused with "in." "Contemporary" is the authentic spirit of the times, just as bare-breasted dancers from hot tropical countries where skin is the height of fashion are authentic. "In" is precious and posturing, trying to put something over on the squares, like topless go-go dancers.

The business world is just waiting for the opening bars of the overture. "Marketing concept" means that instead of making a lot of ballet slippers and looking for Cinderellas who can wear them, you first measure all the feet within reach and make the slippers to fit. "Automation" means that instead of human dancers who occasionally fall into the footlights you have robots who either perform perfectly or go flooey all at once and keep spinning on one toe until they have drilled through the stage into the basement.

Some day I ought to try choreographic definitions in sociology and education, but the terminology there is so rich it wearies me to think about it.

Religion, even without tackling "homoiousian" versus "homoöusian," is too challenging to pass by. Take "dialogue." In the secular, concrete sense, it is the words a copywriter puts on paper for one animated cigarette to speak to the other in a television commercial. Ecumenically speaking, "dialogue" means a give-and-take exchange between partisans of opposed viewpoints. Since this kind of dialogue requires mutual cooperation, it must be danced, as in classical ballet, as a *pas de deux*.

In contrast, "collegiality," with its invitation to expressions of opinion from below, is a conga. Try it. Col-legi-ali-TY. Col-legi-ali-TY. One-two-three-KICK. Of course, not everyone dances out a particular word in the same way. Some quarters (not mentioning any names) interpret "collegiality" as a tarantella, the old Italian dance in which the participants go round in circles till they (or the spectators) drop.

"Relevance." This is a word frequently used in a paragraph suggesting that the Church, in its more bureaucratic aspects, has tried to keep doing the minuet without noticing that the band is now playing rock 'n' roll. "Relevance," in the sense covering the reforms instituted by Vatican II, is danced by some groups as a gallopade, by others as a hesitation waltz.

Two words that confuse many persons who haven't followed developments closely are "charisma" and "kerygma." Their meanings become more accessible if we visualize a big production number in a musical—Broadway, for reasons of taste, not Hollywood.

First, we see the chorus costumed as villagers, serfs and assorted rustics. Enter a stranger in disguise, who, as he leaps and spins, is revealed as a prince. The others gradually fall in line behind him and follow him into the forest to attack the wicked dragon. That's "charisma."

In the next number, the chorus is got up as a band of robbers in another part of the forest (same scenery, to keep the production cost reasonable). The bandits tie up a traveler and fight over his gold, knifing each other in the process. Then the spotlight seeks out one of the dancers, who is seen helping the wounded and freeing the prisoner. Gradually, the other bandits notice his behavior and are confused. As a finale, the charitable bandit dances a soft-shoe routine in which the others join, one by one. That's "kerygma."

All of these words have been current for some time. I suppose many persons already know all the steps. A newer phrase I have noticed only recently is "Christian presence." It seems to be a revised version of "apostolate." The difference is one of mood and tempo. "Apostolate," cued by a fanfare, used to leap in from the wings, kick open the door of the bad baron's dungeon and thrust pamphlets into the arms of the prisoners as they emerged. "Christian presence" is revealed already on-stage as the curtain rises to the accompaniment of soft strings, *dolce*.

The Burning of Rome

Dear Ma: *August* 15

Here I am at Mediatrix of Graces. I'm going to like it here, I think. The pastor, Monsignor Higgins, seems to be a kindly old man. The other assistant is Jim Farrell, whom you may remember. He was two years ahead of me at the seminary. We worked together on the school paper and I always found him good company.

I have a big comfortable room with built-in shelves and cabinets. All the buildings and grounds here are in perfect condition. Jim says that's because we have Stan Gronski, who is probably the best parish janitor in the entire world. Will write more when I get settled.

Don

Dear Ma: *August* 29

I think I mentioned in my last letter that we have the world's best janitor. Well, we also have the WORST house-keeper. Her name is Martha Borg. Jim insists she shortened her name from Borgia because her cooking is so poisonous. The pastor doesn't seem to notice how bad the food is. His health is rather shaky and he scarcely eats anything.

At breakfast the coffee is just tolerable, but the eggs are always overcooked. Eating one of Martha's fried eggs is like munching on a piece of the white rubber raincoat Uncle Pat used to wear when he was a fire marshal. For lunch she puts out a plate of sandwiches. You wouldn't think anything could go wrong with sandwiches, but hers are just a piece of bologna slapped between two naked pieces of bread with no butter. And the bread is stale.

Dinner is invariably a conglomeration of leftovers. I have not yet figured this out. When other women serve leftovers there is an original roast or something for the leftovers to be left over from. Martha puts out leftovers *en casserole* night after night without ever showing us the original. Jim's theory is that she has been practicing the multiplication of loaves and fishes bit and can't quite get it right.

Fortunately, Jim has tipped me off on his survival techniques. Martha doesn't mind snacks in the kitchen as long as we clean up afterwards. So Jim gets up early enough to beat Martha to the kitchen and make his own egg. (Because of the pastor's health, Jim has been able to juggle the parish Mass schedule to make this convenient for himself.) At lunch he reconstructs his sandwiches with butter, pickles, and whatever else is needed to offset the staleness of the bread. He sits through dinner as a courtesy to the pastor, but doesn't eat any. Later in the evening, after Martha has retired to her TV, he fixes himself a three or four-course "snack." From now on Jim and I will both eat better with less effort because we'll take turns doing the cooking.

If you can see your way clear to send us some of your homemade bread from time to time, I can guarantee it won't be wasted.

Don

Dear Ma: *September 18*

Thank you for the bread. It helped Jim and me survive a mysterious week when Martha served leftovers from the left-overs!

I've been spending much of my time lately working with the young people. They're good kids but so bubbling over with wild energy that coping with them wears me out.

Stan Gronski and a couple of men in the parish built a beautiful club room in the school basement for the high school crowd's meetings and parties. All the storage is built in. Even the ping pong table folds up and slides into a slot in the wall. Stan says he likes things neat.

This led to a funny misunderstanding. The kids collected a big pile of used sports equipment—outgrown ice skates, baseball mitts and the like—to send to the inner city. We needed boxes to pack it in so I went around to stores in town collecting empty cartons. I had to go to three stores to find enough; boxes are hard to come by nowadays. When I returned, some eighth grade boys hanging around after school volunteered to help carry in the boxes for me. I guess they just dumped them on the floor in the club room without telling Stan where the boxes had come from or what they were for. By the time I came in with the last armload, Stan already had shoved all my other boxes into the incinerator. He said cardboard boxes lying around are a fire hazard.

So I had to make a quick trip to four more stores. I didn't mind too much. In the end it was worth it to see the enthusiasm of the kids who packed the stuff at our end—and heart-warming to see the pleasure of the kids at the other end who got it to play with.

Don

Dear Ma: *September 21*

Monsignor Higgins is a surprising man. I knew he was good-hearted and well-meaning. I didn't expect him to be so knowing and sympathetic about the new trends in the Church. We had a long meeting last night in the rectory to discuss ways of revitalizing the parish in the spirit of Vatican II. He had a whole page of ideas written out.

I'm to start work right away on improving the congregational singing at the Sunday Masses and organizing a questionnaire to be sent to every family in the parish.

Jim says the old man would do much more if he had the

strength. As it is, he stirs things up whenever he gets to feeling a little better than usual.

I've already selected a list of hymns I'm sure the people will find easier and more appealing than what they're used to. Right now I have to go type out the words on a stencil so we can mimeograph several hundred copies before Sunday.

It will take hours to finish the job. Jim says our machine is so old it could have run off the first copies of the Ten Commandments. It's very temperamental and would have stopped working years ago but for the mechanical genius of Mr. Gronski.

Don

Dear Ma: *September 28*

We are a whole week behind on our music program. When I went to Jim's earliest Mass Sunday expecting to start teaching the new hymns, all my copies of the words had disappeared from the back of the church where I put them myself the night before.

Stan had burned them!

When I asked him why he was so hasty about shoveling everything into his incinerator, he merely shrugged and said loose paper is a fire hazard.

This is going to be a rough weekend. Monsignor Higgins is taking a vacation in Arizona. On top of all the usual activities, I have to republish the hymn sheets, give an evening of recollection for the young people and draft a list of questions for the questionnaire.

Don

Dear Ma: *October 16*

Jim and I need the strength we are getting from your home-made bread. Poor Monsignor Higgins hasn't come back from Arizona. His health took a turn for the worse and the doctors advised him to stay out there until he feels better. They say the climate is good for him. Back at the Mediatrix of Graces ranch, Jim and I have to do everything.

I'm just now getting around to tackling the questionnaire. Although I've never done anything like this before, I think I know what a good parish questionnaire should do. It should have provocative questions to draw out the people, open end questions to give them a chance to express themselves honestly.

The singing on Sunday is picking up, especially at the Masses most of my young people attend. They know all the words by heart from helping me make copies of the hymn sheets.

There's one advantage to having the pastor away. Jim has tactfully suggested a few changes in menu to La Borgia. Wednesday night we had steaks sliced off a truck tire and Thursday night polar bear liver and bacon. Not exactly French cuisine but better than leftovers of leftovers.

Don

Dear Ma: *October 24*

For better or worse, the questionnaire has been mailed. I'll be interested to see how the people respond to this first experience of collegiality at the parish level.

Meanwhile, I have my hands full with the young people. Some of them broke into the club room last night and held an unauthorized party. To make it worse, they were drinking beer. But, as Stan pointed out when he cleaned up this morning, at least they were neat. They put the beer cans in the trash receptacle instead of leaving them strewn around.

I don't know what to do about it. If we don't make some response, they'll think they can get away with anything. On the other hand, only a few of the kids were involved. I think I know who they were (the usual trouble-makers), but I have no proof.

Jim says they wouldn't have dared pull a stunt like that with Monsignor Higgins in town.

Don

Dear Ma: November 15

Now that the questionnaire returns are mostly in, I can see I was mistaken about a lot of things. One mistake was supposing the laity was ready for responsible participation in the life of the parish. Many of their comments are just plain stupid.

One lady objected to the fact that the church steps get wet when it rains or snows. Another yawp complained he can't find a seat at the 11:30 Mass unless he gets there on time.

About two hundred of them wanted the 10:15 Mass changed to 10:30. Another couple of hundred wanted it at 10 o'clock sharp.

Some answers were intelligent and constructive, but even more were actually vicious.

This may have been partly my fault. The questions I tried hardest to make provocative were the ones that seemed to pull the most responses from people with grudges. We heard from a man whose uncle was refused burial in a Catholic cemetery in 1932. Several women gave detailed accounts of their marital problems, which they blamed on the Church's birth control teachings. We filled a whole box with complaints about rhythm.

The next most widespread gripe was about money. This one is worth quoting: "You priests got your nerve standing up in the pulpit asking for money Sunday after Sunday from we working people. You sit in your rectery (sic) eating rich food and taking it easy while people like me are out slaving for our dollars." We would have liked to send that man one of Martha's cakes, but that would have been uncharitable.

Jim says the only public mention of money at Mediatrix of Graces during his time has been the pastor's financial report once a year. Monsignor Higgins has always been an easy-going pastor. He's coming back from Arizona and Jim is afraid the questionnaire returns will break his heart. So many of the comments are unfriendly and unfair.

They even lashed out at the world's best parish janitor: "I mow my own grass when I come home from work. Why don't

you priests mow your own grass? Then you wouldn't need to
pay all that money for a custodian."

It's funny, in a way, but sad, too. Pray for us.

Don

Dear Ma: *November* 20

I suppose I sounded discouraged in my last letter. You'll be
pleased to know the general situation has improved. The Monsignor is back, looking tanned and—for him—healthy. The rest
in Arizona did him good.

After all our worry, the problem of the questionnaire returns
solved itself. Jim and I had sorted them into piles in the
rectory basement where there was plenty of room. Some of the
most numerous categories were in boxes. And there was one
whole box of late returns that hadn't been opened yet.

All of this disappeared the day before Monsignor Higgins returned. It seems that Mr. Gronski came down to the rectory
basement to recharge the water softener for Martha. He saw
what I have to admit was a rather disorderly array of papers
and boxes. Within minutes every last scrap was in the incinerator.

When we found out what had happened. I was furious at
first. Jim soon had me laughing. He said this was the best
thing that could have happened, pointing out that the pastor
feels virtuously collegial, having authorized the exploration of
parishioners' feelings. However, he has been spared reading the
distressing results. An act of God.

As for my young people, there's something about the Monsignor's presence that awes them. I wish I had the knack. The
ringleader came to him, confessed all, promised never again to
sneak beer into the club room and obtained forgiveness. I've
already noticed a more cooperative spirit among the whole
group.

The only cloud on the horizon is La Borgia's cooking, which

is worse than ever (if that's possible). You can't imagine how much I am looking forward to YOUR cooking on Thanksgiving. See you Thursday.

Don

Everyman Ecumenist

(A MORALITY PLAY)

Not too many years ago, Catholics and Protestants would rather have received information embarrassing to the other side than strike oil in the pastor's garden.

"Aha," the Protestants would say when some evidence of highhandedness on the part of Catholic clergy would come to light, "the usual Popish tyranny!"

"Phooey to you, too," the Catholics would retort when next they snatched a distinguished convert from the bosom of do-it-yourself heresy.

In an incredibly short time, all this has changed. Catholics and Protestants now sit down together and good-humoredly confess their shortcomings. It appears that both sides are well supplied with anecdotal material. In fact, with typical American competitiveness, we are now playing the ecumenical form of "Can You Top This?" Any number can play, as long as two or more denominations are represented. The game goes like this:

CATHOLIC: You Protestants are lucky. Your clergy are trained to give good sermons. Our Father Brown is a wonderful person but his sermons are a penance.

PROTESTANT: Good sermons? Good grief! Our minister is so fond of the sound of his voice that he runs on like a tape recorder. You could slice any one of his sermons into pieces and get enough to last every Sunday for months. It's you Catholics who are lucky. Everything is done for you. We have to hire our own clergy, raise funds and administer the property.

CATHOLIC: But at least you have something to say about how your money is spent. In our last parish, the pastor thought the Depression was still on. He wouldn't spend a penny on repairs until something fell over. When the church roof started to leak, he merely moved the baptismal font under the place and blessed the water as it accumulated.

PROTESTANT: But your new church is so beautiful inside. Ours looks like a funeral parlor with a pulpit.

CATHOLIC: I'm glad you mentioned the arts. You have a professional minister of music who has trained a splendid choir. Our organist and choir are no closer to finding the lost chord now than they were five years ago.

This is what ecumenical dialogue sounds like at the grassroots level. If the Catholics bet on one priest sent to South America to shut him up, the Protestants take the pot with two segregated congregations in the South and a minister fired by his trustees for supporting peace and civil rights.

Several times I nearly have been trounced at this game by Protestants armed with "God is dead" theologians. But, so far, some Catholic prelate in Italy or South America has always turned up with a statement outrageous enough to give me ammunition for a return volley.

Many of the leaders on both sides who encouraged the ecumenical dialogue hoped that in the process Catholics and Protestants would learn valuable techniques from each other for coping with common problems. In some ways, this has worked out. The Methodist Church in South Platypus, Nebraska, with uniformed Knights of Columbus directing traffic, set a new record by serving 38,734 chicken dinners in three hours and twelve minutes.

On balance, we all seem to have learned more about what

DOESN'T work. In Catholic circles, the more enthusiastic liturgists were optimistic about the results of changing the language of the mass to the language of the people. At the time, an Anglican clergyman advised us not to expect too much. While agreeing that the change was a needed reform, he observed that his church had worshiped in the vernacular for 400 years without moving many mountains.

Catholics concerned about the future of the parochial school system and the apparent ineffectiveness of many Confraternity of Christian Doctrine programs have been eyeing the Protestant Sunday schools. Since they seem to have maintained the vitality of Protestantism in this country generation after generation, they must be doing something right.

But the Protestants don't think so. They are criticizing their own Sunday schools as ineffective and irrelevant. The Reverend William A. Morrison, General Secretary of the Board of Christian Education of the United Presbyterian Church, publicly complained that in too many churches the Sunday school is scheduled to conflict with the hour of worship, making school and church "competitors rather than colleagues." He thinks families ought to worship together.

Catholics will recognize this argument as similar to the winning side of the controversy about special children's masses a few years ago.

Protestants sometimes yearn for a little Catholic discipline. I was at an ecumenical meeting one night when clergymen began discussing methods for maintaining church membership in a mobile community where about one-third of the families move every year. The Protestants compared notes on such devices as mailings to new residents and doorbell-ringing teams of laymen. Then they turned to a priest and said, "How do the Roman Catholics handle this problem, Father?"

They were stunned when he said his parish did nothing whatever to recruit new families; Catholics moving into a new parish automatically register at the rectory. The ministers, who obviously are never free of the struggle to maintain a flock, could scarcely imagine a congregation into which the replacements fall like manna from heaven.

If Father felt a twinge of temptation to smugness, it soon passed. The next topic was per capita performance at the collection basket, in which Protestants could bury us. (And not in silver.)

I am told also that some Protestants are interested in the Catholic approach to the liturgical cycle. In contrast to the days when the Puritans were so strongly anti-holiday that they would not celebrate Christmas, Protestants have said they see value in relating life to worship day by day.

Meanwhile, back at the chancery office, Catholics are quietly dropping holy days. In areas where Catholic children ride the same buses as public school children, the Catholic schools hold class on holy days in order not to disrupt the bus schedule. Catholic organizations open their offices for business as usual on holy days. "Now that we pay fair salaries, competitive with business generally, we don't have to give our employees holy days off as a fringe benefit," I was told by the head of one large Catholic organization.

Any day, I expect to hear about the formation of a group to be called "Protestants and Others United to Keep the Catholics from Going Overboard." A friend of mine has been talking about organizing POUKCGO himself if he has to.

I think it's partly because he's a poor loser. He thought he had me topped with a small-town scandal about a minister who left his wife and eloped with a soprano from the choir, but I mowed him down with a whole batch of married ex-priests and nuns who had defected at least partly as a form of protest.

My friend stated his complaint this way: "How can I be a Protestant if I can't tell what I'm protesting against without reading the newspapers every morning to find out what the Catholics are protesting against? Maybe we'll get up some morning and we'll all be protesting about exactly the same things. Then we won't be able to play 'Can You Top This?' any more."

Let's Take It Again
from the Top, Sister

As part of the new involvement of nuns in society, at least one sister has become a member of the Actors Equity Association. Conservative Catholics need not yet avoid the theater for fear of seeing a nun with her instep exposed in some shocking new play. In the case mentioned, the sister established her eligibility for Actors Equity as a director rather than a performer.

It should not surprise us that nuns are taking an interest in the theater. After all, the Church was once Europe's leading impresario—sponsoring the miracle plays that kept drama alive during the Middle Ages. In fact, one sometimes gets the impression from reading the history of the period that much of what went on was planned with the eventual movie version in mind. The Crusades alone have provided employment for countless extras. Several kings and popes seem to have deliberately conducted themselves as if they hoped they would someday be portrayed by Laurence Olivier or Richard Burton.

If a nun with theatrical know-how could have been in charge, she might have cast John Wayne as Harold at the Battle of Hastings with profound effect on the course of history. The picture would have to have an ending with box office appeal, so William (played by Jack Palance) and his Normans would have lost instead of won.

As convent and show-biz influences mingle in the future, we can look for the development of a new culture, just as the collision of Norman and Saxon ways created a new people in England. The first repercussions may be felt in the financing of stage productions. Costs have risen so much that any show not instantly acclaimed a hit is a flop, in contrast to the past when it was possible for a show to be only moderately successful and still enjoy a run.

If this trend continues, nuns may be the only persons in the country with enough skill at fund-raising to collect sufficient backing for new theatrical productions. They'll get most of it a nickel at a time from school children. The rest will come a million at a time from tough businessmen with bad consciences, whom no one but nuns could turn into "angels."

Of course, if the nuns raise the money, they'll control the show. When curtain time is 8:00 P.M., the audience will have to be in their seats no later than 7:00. No talking will be allowed during intermission. Anyone chewing gum will be required to bring a note from his mother before being admitted to the third act.

A sure sign that convent influence is making itself felt in show business will be the complete disappearance of movies in which nuns play baseball and ride motorcycles.

As for theatrical influences on nuns, we must not be scandalized when we see flashy techniques being used in unexpected quarters.

Press agentry. The Mother Superior of the order comes to town on business, so the newspaper photo desk is routinely notified: "Mother M. Bibiana arriving American Flight 321 4:00 P.M. Tuesday. Will discuss plans for giant *première* of new social service center. In hospital maternity department, babies' footprints will be recorded upon arrival in concrete floor."

News will be leaked to the gossip columnists: "Mother M. Bibiana apparently has patched up her feud with officials of a certain diocese. Last year, she cut back the number of teachers assigned to that diocese from her order by twenty per cent and the order's marching band cancelled its scheduled appearance at the new cathedral dedication. This department has just learned that although the marching band has been booked for a European tour during the coming season, the order's combo will be allowed to play a series of benefit jazz masses."

Plugola. The economics of broadcasting are based on the fact that publicity has so much value celebrities can be dragged in front of TV cameras for little or no payment and made to like it. Many theatrical personalities spend more time promoting their productions through guest appearances than actually performing.

Already we are seeing nuns on television. Since nuns by definition have something to promote, we can expect them to take over more and more channels in the future, as the benefits of plugola become better known to the less progressive orders.

"You're here in town, Sister, to build a new home for retired actresses who played the roles of nuns?"

"That's right, Buck. Some of them spent so many years with *The Sound of Music* that they'll feel more at home in our kind of atmosphere now that they've left the theater."

"I'm sure the people of this city will help you as generously as they can. Folks, I'll tell you where to send your contribution right after this next message from our sponsor. . . ."

Don't be surprised when *Variety* starts publishing the results of fund drives along with box-office reports.

Theatrical unions. That sister who joined Actors Equity probably didn't realize what she's starting. If such organizations of firm purpose as the American Federation of Television and Radio Artists or the Screen Actors Guild ever get a foothold, convent life will be quite different.

We cut now to the Convent of St. Debbie in Hollywood, California. The Mother Superior is about to read a letter aloud. She asks one of the younger sisters to move the lamp closer.

"I'd love to do it for you, Mother, but I'll have to find Sister Gertrude. She belongs to the stagehand's union."

"That's not right," interrupts another sister. "Moving a lamp that's lit is a job for the grip. Where's Sister Rose?"

"Never mind," says the Mother Superior. "I'll scoot my chair closer to the lamp."

"Does that count as a rehearsal?" says Sister Joan, the business agent. "You can't be too careful. Rehearsals are time-and-a-half on odd-numbered Thursdays."

"That's all right; if it runs more than thirteen weeks, I get residuals," the superior snaps back absently. Then she remembers what she was doing. "Wait a minute. I'm only trying to read you this letter. It's from one of our fans in Rome."

"You can read it as long as you do it off camera," says Sister Joan.

Sister Gertrude joins the group. "A fan in Rome. How exciting. What does he say? Easy there, darling, don't touch that lamp."

"I can't make out a couple of these words—it's in Latin—but I gather he wants to know when we're going to cut another platter."

"Not till next year," says Sister Joan. "We get a tax break if we hold off."

Sister Rose enters. "May I have that Vatican City stamp for my collection?"

The Mother Superior tears it off for her. "Who can write him an acknowledgment?"

Sister Joan answers. "We don't have anyone of the moment who belongs to any of the writers' guilds. I guess we're stuck."

"Pity," says Sister Rose, who has been looking at the letter over the Mother Superior's shoulder. "There must be several of them. In the letter, he keeps saying 'we.'"

Eventually, as sisters continue to influence the theatrical world and vice versa, the perennial problem about church and state is certain to come up again. This may not be clear right off, so I'll explain. With sisters making hit records, appearing on Broadway, and taking over movies and television, one of them will see her name move from the marquee to the ballot. She'll be drafted to run for the U. S. Senate from California. They think like that in California.

It will be interesting to see how the other senators react to being asked for a contribution to the missions every day.

The Beards of a Prophet

More priests of the Latin Rite should wear beards. A bearded Latin clergy would dramatize the new bonds with the traditionally bewhiskered Orthodox. Also, a beard gives any man poise and presence he might otherwise lack, enhances his fatherly image and gives him something to do with his hands, if he doesn't smoke. He can stroke his beard.

Beardedness long has been an issue in my own family. Scarcely a month goes by without one of the children asking me why I don't grow a beard. I think this preoccupation with the hair on my chin has something to do with the disappearance of hair from my head. The fact is, although the children haven't noticed, I have grown many beards.

The most recent was the flower of a sojourn at a beach cottage on the shores of Lake Michigan. We could have been on a tropical isle. The surf rolled in day after day warm and gentle. The wide beach of golden sand contained few pebbles. Even beer cans were rather scarce.

Sailing, swimming and sunning, I felt far removed from my usual world. Naturally, I began to grow a Beachcomber Beard. It was to be wild, untamed, as free as driftwood following the wind. But on Sunday morning, before mass, I shaved it off.

That was the second beard that year. In the spring I had stayed home from the office several days with assorted respiratory ailments—cold, flu, pneumonia, silicosis and, I think, a touch of Dutch elm. I began a Protest Beard. I could think of any number of things to protest. The more important issues— civil rights, the peace movement and so on—were in good hands, so I thought I would protest elevators with piped-in music, restaurants that try to seat strangers at your table if you lunch alone and parishes that pass the collection basket at confirmation and graduation ceremonies.

Unfortunately, when I shaved off my Protest Beard the following Sunday, I had not had the opportunity to protest anything except that someone had finished my crossword puzzle while I was taking a nap.

The beard before that one was a Creative Beard. This beard style tapers neatly to a point and is most effective with a matching mustache. It identifies the wearer as a creative worker —artist, writer, or perhaps the musical director of a recording company. Devil-may-care, but in the main stream where the big money swims. I probably should have persevered with that beard. It might have been worth a dollar a hair to me in added annual income.

I started my Creative Beard on a Sunday, expecting to get it well started during a week of vacation to follow. But an urgent writing project came along unexpectedly and I absent-mindedly shaved clean the next day while thinking about my work.

Within the family, opinion on my beards is divided. There is a pro-beard faction that is counterbalanced by the anti-beard forces. From time to time one child or another will change sides, but the balance of power remains undisturbed. That is because I am always in favor of a beard and my wife is always against it.

At one time I considered compromising on a mustache. A ripe, full mustache projects plenty of dignity, especially if the ends turn up. I admire the Daliesque mustache with long, spiky points. This model has made Salvator Dali an international celebrity.

A mustache can be an unsatisfactory half-measure. In our conformist society, a mustache is just far enough out to make you uncomfortable without bestowing the majesty that comes with a full beard. For instance, I know of an advertising agency creative director who was trying to hire a copywriter. A friend phoned with a recommendation. The friend said, "This guy's a good writer, but keep your eye on him. He'll be angling for your job after the first week."

Pause. "Know anything else about him?"

"Well, he wears a mustache."

"O.K., send him over. If he's as good as you say, I'll hire him. I can handle anybody with hair on his face."

Whether that creative director would have felt as confident of maintaining his position against a writer who could back his talent with a Creative Beard that had reached its glorious full growth is doubtful.

I don't think the Creative Beard will last long as a pre-eminent style. Until recently, any kind of beard was unemployable in the more conservative fields such as banking, real estate, insurance, law and the like. But I saw a Creative Beard on La Salle Street the other day in front of the Board of Trade. The wearer looked like a bond salesman. Obviously, it's only a matter of time until the "in" people won't tolerate a Creative Beard on a pet poodle.

What style will replace it? That's difficult to guess. I don't think there'll be much interest in the Goatee, which is now sported by certain free spirits who have dropped out of the middle class. Nobody with a Goatee, except a jazz musician, could possibly make more than $7500 a year, and wearers of Creative Beards have been living higher that that.

If I had to choose, I'd bet my razor on Burnsides. I don't think I've ever seen a full set of sidewhiskers except in a daguerreotype. Their novelty makes them attractive. Besides, I have always considered Burnsides a cut of whisker that achieves masculine dignity without being as overbearing as a full bush.

That was why I almost became a taste-maker several years ago. We were spending our vacation in a cabin that was rather primitive. There was no place to plug in my electric razor, so with pleasurable anticipation I set out to grow Burnsides.

Then came Sunday. Plans were made to follow mass with a festive breakfast in a restaurant with white tablecloths, to make up to certain family members for the plainness of our accom-

modations at the cabin. I had to part with my Burnsides in the
bathroom of a filling station.

These are some of the reasons I maintain that more priests
of the Latin Rite should wear beards. If even Father were
waggling a beaver in church, I'd have the nerve to get by that
crucial first Sunday without shaving. I'd have a beard of my
own.

Who Put the Bomb
in Father Murphy's Chowder?

Catholics in England have been arguing about freedom of expression in the Church. The controversy was set off by the re-
moval of a Dominican editor for a strongly worded editorial.
When Patrick Wall, a Conservative Member of Parliament,
participated in a public debate on the subject, he took the conservative side and wondered how much longer the Church could
"stand up to subversion from within."

This was the first time I heard the post-conciliar ferment in
the Church described in Cold War terms. I suddenly realized
I had not understood what was going on. I thought we were
supposed to be arguing, struggling and thinking our way through
the highly debatable questions posed by Vatican II. Now I see
that we have to choose one side or the other in the battle between—I almost said "sheep and goats," but that's old-fashioned
terminology—the subversive, rebellious, corrupted-by-modern-
art Left and the authoritarian, nostalgic-for-the-Inquisition
Right.

Yes, it's all much clearer now. For example, when bishops
object to priests coming in from other dioceses to take part in

various protest movements, they are merely reacting to the classic pattern of Leftist infiltration. One diocese has already established a fortified hamlet program: ushers frisk you at the church door to see if you are carrying a copy of *Commonweal* or the *National Catholic Reporter*.

Liberal dioceses have a different problem. The C.I.A. (Catholic Intransigents Associated) pours in money to provide arms for reactionary groups to attack the diocesan government with full-page ads in newspapers. The priests are continually bothered by airplanes flying overhead and taking pictures to see if anyone is saying experimental masses that are too experimental.

Numerous formerly inexplicable incidents fall neatly into place. You probably remember when a certain Father McCarthy publicly declared that he held in his hand a list of traitors in the chancery office who not only were soft on celibacy but had also been secretly trained abroad by Dutch theologians. Fortunately, a subsequent investigation proved that the chancery office staff—it was a small diocese—consisted entirely of three aged monsignors who had been out of the country only once in their lives, when they had accompanied a previous bishop to the Council of Trent.

Then there was the case of the defecting theologian. He graduated first in his class at West Point Seminary and rose rapidly to command a project in nuclear metaphysics. One morning—possibly because security forces were closing in on him —everyone was shocked to read that he had gone over to the Other Side, taking with him a complete set of top-secret plans for remodeling St. Peter's.

Some papers printed a different version of this episode, but that was because they had not learned to view such things from the Cold War perspective.

The question now is whether the conflict will escalate. One side is alarmed because the other has already encircled so many Catholic publications. And the continuous flow of infiltrators is hard to control because many of them are nuns in secular clothes who look just like non-combatants. Lack of control over the countryside may lead to counterattacks on such hitherto privileged sanctuaries as the Catholic Press Association and the novitiates.

The Council's teachings on collegiality have been interpreted in some quarters as a call for free elections, preferably supervised by an impartial international commission. Others fear that collegiality will revive the Popular Front technique of subversion. It is rumored that in one large diocese where laymen recently held a congress to organize themselves they all turned up at the meeting wearing red shirts. The explanation—that it was a new liturgical idea and they wore red because Pentecost was coming—did not satisfy some observers.

Most people, of course, are aware only of what's going on in their own parish. It is difficult for them to keep track of the day-by-day progress of the global struggle. To find out what the man in the pew is thinking, I toured a number of parishes with the best possible guide—an organ repairman. As a disguise, I wore a green beret.

First we visited a conservative parish. Some of the keys on the organ had to be replaced because the organist had worn them out always playing the same tunes. I was told the pastor reprinted John Birch Society literature in the parish bulletin. The altar not only didn't face the people, it had a rood screen in front of it.

"What do people here think of that?" I asked the housekeeper.

"Hard to say," she replied. "Folks here come to church with their armor on and it's hard to judge what a man is thinking when he has his visor pulled down over his face."

At the next parish we found an owl living in the organ. They hardly played the organ any more, having organized a steel drum band instead. In fact, they didn't use the church itself very often since most masses were being said at someone's house.

I questioned some women I found addressing envelopes for the priests' union. "Do you like the new ways better?"

"Some things, yes; but the steel band is terrible."

To fill out the picture, I also interviewed a correspondent who has seen many of the leading trouble spots first hand. "It's all more confusing than the public realizes," he told me. "For instance, among the Leftists there is a considerable force of revisionists. The revisionists say that not all the old ways have to be thrown out, that it is just possible the Church has been right about some things during the past 2,000 years."

I asked whether he had talked to moderate conservatives. "Of course. And you'd be surprised how many are willing to negotiate if the enemy will only stop saying you can't trust anybody over thirty."

So there may be hope for a peaceful settlement yet.

I, Thou, He, She, It, They and Them

In days of yore people had coarser faults. My illustrious ancestor, Sir Richard Coeur de Goat, would occasionally fly into a rage and cleave a neighbor to the wishbone with a sword. According to family tradition, he once became infatuated with a pretty damozel who lived in a neighboring castle. One dark night he butted down the gate with his bare head and abducted her.

Later in life, he sincerely repented of his misdeeds and tried to atone for them with an equal lack of subtlety. Joining a passing crusade, he walked to the Holy Land barefoot and piously slaughtered Saracens in heaps until his luck ran out. While wearing his hair shirt, he was mistaken by a nearsighted archer for an enemy camel and felled with an arrow.

This is an example of how spiritual styles change. People don't take to the extreme asceticism of former times. Anyone today who sat on the top of a pole like Simeon Stylites would be thought to be advertising something. Sackcloth has lost its symbolic force. Any attempt to revive it probably would result in a run on sackcloth by the fashion industry. Pilgrimages haven't died out entirely, but with champagne dinners on the first-class flights they aren't what they used to be.

In the history of Christianity, the first of the spiritual styles was martyrdom. It didn't do the early Christians any good to talk themselves blue in the face. The Romans were used to that. One of their subject tribes, the Britons, topped it by painting themselves blue all over. But the Romans found the steadfastness of the martyrs convincing. The more outrageous the persecution, the more the martyrs won public support—even without newspapers to print photographs of the cattle prods and police dogs.

The martyrs were so successful it was natural for later Christians to honor them. In time it was overdone. I, for instance, am not inspired to become a better and nobler man by the big toe of St. Malfortunatus.

Malfortunatus was walking along the street in Rome one day minding his own business. He turned a corner and ran smack into a group of young zealots who were chanting, "Cohort brutality, cohort brutality." Troops surrounded the area and shoved everyone they caught, including Malfortunatus, into a long black chariot with barred windows. Although he was not one of the demonstrators, he was indeed a Christian who refused to worship the Emperor, who at that time was somebody's horse.

It didn't matter that Malfortunatus had been walking along minding his own business; they cut him up in small pieces and tried to feed him to the lions anyway. But the lions had been overworked that week. They finally couldn't eat another bite. If Malfortunatus had been standing farther back in the line, he might have escaped entirely. As it was, the lions called a wildcat strike and walked off the job before his big toe had been processed.

Other Christian prisoners who were released (to give the lions a rest) took the toe with them and built a shrine for it. Miraculously, its toenail kept growing. The nail was kept trimmed, and the cuttings were widely used as a remedy for gout. To this day, the toe is said to be able to point to anyone in the room who has not always minded his own business. Since the toe points at anyone who comes to see it, I think we can assume this claim is true. Nevertheless, it doesn't inspire me.

Later on, when Christianity had taken over the Empire, many were so scandalized at what went on in the cities even in a Christian milieu that they withdrew to the desert. Alone in the wilderness, they developed an ascetic style that was both rigorous and spectacular. Crowds came out to see them. Two of the best known were Milton Burro and Gopher Pyle.

Milton Burro was distinguished for his austerities. One of his favorites was running barefoot through a cactus patch. He said the cacti symbolized the prickings of the human conscience. It was his custom to be buried alive for varying periods. "There's nothing like being buried from time to time to remind you of the brevity of life," he wrote. Just after the last time he was buried, a civil war broke out in the province. By the time order was restored and his friends could come back to dig him up, they had forgotten the exact spot.

Gopher Pyle was noted more for his sage advice than for his dramatic penances, although it probably wasn't much fun living as he did in the same cave with a surly bear and a nest of asps. Distinguished men of his times, discouraged by the course of events, would pilgrimage to his cave to meditate and learn from his wisdom. The Emperor Theodolite, for one, should have paid closer attention. "If I were you, Ted," Gopher told him, "I'd kick that baggage, the Empress, out of the palace right now." But the Emperor paid no heed, and within six months the Empress had poisoned him and married one of his generals.

Sometimes, trying to write in a household where the nine other residents seem chiefly occupied with playing musical instruments and re-enacting the Fort Dearborn Massacre, I feel a certain attraction for the desert life. The hermit part. I don't think I'd get much out of walking barefoot through the cacti. I must admit, however, that when some friends of mine in Arizona put a chunk of cholla on my chair just before I sat down, I did find the experience uplifting.

Another style of Christianity that seems to have coexisted with others from an early date without flowering until recent centuries is anti-intellectualism. I remember being attracted to it myself in college after a disastrous chemistry examination. It was best expressed by François Fflunque, a simple country priest who wrote a spiritual treatise advising his readers to scorn worldly knowledge.

"If someone accost thee with intent to tell thee some New Thing, he is probably the Devil in disguise; send him away.

"If the Book-of-the-Month Club deposit a volume on thy doorstep, it is a trap for thy soul; take that treacherous volume out of doors and burn it, along with all accumulated Book Dividend certificates.

"You have no need of the kind of worldly knowledge that occupies the learned doctors in the universities, where they still think the world is flat anyway."

Unlike anti-intellectualism, which still has many adherents, mysticism seems to have suffered something of a decline. One of the last mystics with unusual powers was St. Ubiquitus, who mastered bilocation early in his career and had achieved trilocation before he was thirty. St. Ubiquitus developed this specialty to a higher degree than anyone else before or since. During the Mardi Gras celebration of 1571, he divided himself into two groups of twenty each and conducted a tug of war for the amusement of the faithful, Reds against the Blues, which was won by the Blues in one hour nine minutes and forty-three seconds.

I don't mean to suggest that people today are either better or worse than they were when older styles of religion were in vogue. I do think the moderns are more delicately adjusted.

In former times, if you decided to take vengeance on an enemy, the logistics could become quite taxing. First, you had to call up some vassals and make sure everyone had a good spear. A couple of varlets had always lost their spears and had to be given new ones at your expense. Then you had to supply provisions. It was probably some distance to your enemy's manor, and the going and coming would take several days at least.

Once the party was organized, you tried to gain the advantage of surprise by moving only at night. This slowed you down, increased your chances of being knocked off your horse in the dark by the limb of a tree and gave you time to reconsider.

When you finally arrived, chances are they heard you coming miles away anyhow and took shelter in the castle with the drawbridge up. So there was nothing you could do but burn the pig barn, go home and hope for better luck another time.

A person had to be really angry not to cool off while all this was going on.

Nowadays, a full measure of vengeance against an enemy can be accomplished with the lift (or non-lift) of an eyebrow. Let us say that your colleague Joe Crotalus has been appointed to present the department's recommendations at a meeting. At the conclusion of Joe's presentation, the boss looks around the table. You ought to appear interested and give a nod of concurrence since you worked on the report with Joe and furnished a considerable part of its content. Instead you lower your eyes at the note pad in front of you and move one eyebrow no more than a sixteenth of an inch. This clearly conveys that you tried to talk Joe out of the report's conclusions but he insisted on going ahead and making a fool of himself and you're too decent to say anything against the report now.

You have dealt Crotalus (that snake!) a sore wound that may do him more damage than if you had smacked him with a mace. You may in time repent of this deed, but as a product of your own century you won't feel obliged to subsist in the desert for six months on a diet of worms as a penance.

Two new styles of Christianity now seem to be coming to the fore. One concentrates on social action, the other on interpersonal relationships. Neither is a new discovery.

If my ancestor, Sir Richard Coeur de Goat, had not felt enough of a generous twinge on occasion to dabble in social action, people would have taken revenge on him by starving to death under his dining-room windows and spoiling his appetite. In our day the affluent portion of the population wouldn't know such evils as poverty existed if they weren't brought to public attention by reporters and reformers.

Fortunately, there are dedicated persons like Father Mark "Seven-League Boots" Polo. He marches. During the past year alone, he has worn out forty-three pairs of shoes demonstrating for peace, civil rights, collective bargaining for agricultural workers and better poverty programs. Father Polo thinks marching ought to be incorporated into the new liturgy as a natural development of the traditional procession. "A couple of laps around the church would help keep everyone in shape for the next protest."

Although attention to interpersonal relationships was part of Christianity from the beginning, we understand such things better now. We used to talk about "Me and You." Then our immigrant forebears went to night school and learned better grammar: "You and I." After that, Martin Buber taught us to be more sensitive, distinguishing "I and Thou" from "I and It." Some folks agreed, but thought there ought to be room for an "I-You" relationship about halfway between "I-Thou" and "I-It." This makes quite a crowd: You, Thou, It, I and Me, not to mention They and Them (as in "They ought to do something about them bums who hang around this neighborhood"). When this mob assembles in one place, there is multiplicity of being that would strain St. Ubiquitus himself.

I welcome the new styles in religion—as much as anyone can who isn't all that gregarious.

WHERE Did You Say Two or Three Are Gathered Together?

During civil rights demonstrations in Chicago, a New York *Times* correspondent commented on the difference of opinion between clergy and laymen on the question of open housing. Priests and nuns were marching among the demonstrating Negroes while Catholic laymen were throwing rocks and bottles (presumably having first poured the holy water from Lourdes into other containers).

This episode focused national attention on a problem the religious sociologists ought to investigate. We like to think of the Church as moving forward in well-ordered array under a common banner. Over the centuries, it does. But in the short run the principle seems to be that wherever two or three are gathered together they'll immediately march off in several directions.

This is especially true when the individuals belong to different estates. Without theologizing, one can pragmatically divide the Church into three estates—hierarchical, clerical and lay.

The hierarchical estate includes not only bishops and abbots but also others in positions of authority—anyone who can write a valid check against the bank account of a religious not-for-profit corporation. Under this definition Mothers Superior, college presidents and even a few laymen belong to the hierarchical estate.

In the clerical estate, I include the impecunious clergy, most nuns, all seminarians and others who in the ecclesiastical chain of command find it more blessed to receive than to give.

The lay estate is composed of most laymen. This estate can

be subdivided into those who contribute but don't participate, those who participate but don't contribute much, and those who both contribute and participate (generally believed to number exactly 144,000).

There used to be a fourth estate but it has been turned into a retreat house for repentant church architects.

It must not be thought that recriminations can be aimed at any one estate for not falling in with the others. For example, in 1891 Pope Leo XIII issued the encyclical *Rerum Novarum* to combat the ruthlessness and injustice of nineteenth-century capitalism. Did the higher, or example-setting, estates follow him to the barricades?

Henri Daniel-Rops, the distinguished Church historian, regretfully concedes that the higher estates mostly did nothing. "The episcopate as a whole remained undemonstrative, and the clergy, overwhelmingly conservative, reacted in the same way." As for the laity, they didn't even bother to find out what was going on. "Encyclicals commonly go unread by the majority of Catholics," the historian adds, "and *Rerum Novarum* was no exception."

In this case, a pope had a brilliant insight into a social problem and provided effective answers. It took only half a century or so for the various estates to get the message.

Nowadays, of course, we have faster and more efficient means of communication. When the leading members of the hierarchical estate assembled in Rome for the Second Vatican Council, it took scarcely any time at all for the other estates to find out that opinions of the bishops on various questions were far from unanimous. Often accused by outsiders in the past of being monolithic, the Church revealed itself to be as joyfully variegated as the parts bin at a mosaic factory.

These high-level events are documented by journalists and historians. I still want the sociologists to study what happens at the point of contact between the lower clergy and the laity.

Why is it that laymen who bone up on the social encyclicals, the Council documents and current theology always live in a parish where the pastor thinks the Council of Trent was Communist inspired? And why is it that the truly apostolic pastor always finds himself surrounded by parishioners who never participate in anything because they're all too busy trying to get George Washington impeached posthumously?

Perhaps I shouldn't say "always." A friend of mine who knows the Church inside and out (he sells pews and pre-fabricated grottoes) says he has heard of one parish where the clerical estate and the lay estate seem to match fairly well. The priests and the people belong to the same Sicilian clan, which makes them all cousins.

But even under the most favorable conditions, a certain lack of understanding between priests and laymen probably is inevitable.

An activist layman tends to talk big and offer to fight City Hall. Suppose, in support of some worthwhile cause with moral overtones, his pastor joins him in a civic battle. At the height of the ruckus, when the community is well stirred up, the layman may take a promotion from his company and be transferred to another city. Left behind to finish the battle, smooth things over with the mayor, soothe ruffled parishioners and explain matters to the bishop is the familiar figure in the well-worn cassock.

The layman necessarily leads a considerable part of his life out of touch with the institutional Church. He can never become as totally involved as the priest.

At the same time, a priest can easily overlook or minimize a layman's commitment to his family. Sometimes this takes the form of encouraging the joiners (who don't need encouragement) to be out nights when they really ought to be spending more time at home. Or, when a layman excuses himself for family reasons from some joint enterprise, the priest may be too easily reminded of the Scriptural ingrates who turned down invitations to the feast.

So the layman wonders why some of his schemes arouse little

enthusiasm at the rectory. And the priest shakes his head over the laymen who seem uncommitted and undependable.

In the long run, all this probably is just as well. It keeps us from making mistakes. Historically, when a high percentage of the members of the Church started marching in the same direction at the same time, all three estates united, they likely as not had something in mind that wasn't exactly edifying.

Consider the Fourth Crusade. Pope Innocent III preached it. Bishops, abbots and priests spread the word. Laymen turned out, sword in hand. But none of them ever set foot in the Holy Land. Instead, they went to Constantinople and swiped it from the Greeks.

The Draft in the Upper Room

Now that the newspapers have begun to give religious news even more space than the curling matches, I have become aware of a pessimistic outlook among clergymen which I never noticed before. It used to be that clerical statements on the growth of church membership sounded almost like a booster message from the Chamber of Commerce. Next year will be better. A few minutes a day of your time will change the world. Our radio broadcasts are bringing the Gospel to every grass hut in Africa. Since there are no atheists in foxholes and all the men in the country have been in foxholes in one war or another, we can anticipate a great religious revival. The latest census figures show that We are gaining on the Others. The Catholic press makes converts. All we need now is a new wing on the seminary and—

They don't talk like this any more. Now those who make public comments on the prospects of religion seem to vie with each other to paint the blackest picture. (They do it with red ink.)

To make certain that matters were not being exaggerated by the sensation-mongering press, I called on several leading prophets to get the facts firsthand. My first interview was with Dr. Robert MacTavish Plaid, a Protestant noted for his ecumenical contacts with Catholics. I found him hoeing potatoes in front of his parsonage. The spacious grounds of parsonage and church had been turned into a truck farm.

"It's going to be rough," Dr. Plaid said. "In the old days people joined our church because it was the thing to do. We didn't make too many demands on them—pay your pew rent on time, send the kids to Sunday school and no bingo playing. I didn't see a lot of burning faith around, but plenty of folks thought there might be something to religion and they'd better play it safe and go along, since it wasn't much trouble. Now that we're taking stands on moral issues and it's becoming harder to be a Christian, I'm afraid there's going to be no one left but those who are really convinced."

"You don't think that's many, sir?" I asked.

Dr. Plaid waved his hoe at the crops. "Well, with the garden here and a few dollars from renting the church out a couple of nights a week I hope to hold out for a while."

A similar view was expressed by Monsignor Jeremiah O'Pshaw, pastor of a large Catholic parish. He feared that the new emphasis on performing positive acts of charity instead of, as formerly, avoiding the pains of Hell by not eating meat on Friday would weaken the faithful.

"We used to catch them young in school," he said. "By the time they graduated from eighth grade they were so scared they could almost feel the flames.

"One Sunday a tornado picked the church up and set it down across the river in the next county. Would you believe it? Despite the inconvenience, we had only eight parishioners who dared miss turning up in their pews in time for ten o'clock mass. And that was because a house fell on them. Sometimes

I think a little fear was a good thing. It helped fill the church on Sunday."

"Do you think religious sentiment is waning?"

"Definitely. Consider our men's club and our women's club. They used to take turns packing the church basement for programs on football or flower arranging. They'd charge a small admission fee and make a donation to the church. Now they schedule adult education classes on Scripture or theology and the hall's so empty you could do a rerun of the destruction of Sodom and Gomorrah without ruffling anyone's hair."

"Is the ecumenical movement having an effect one way or another?"

"Indeed, yes. Our women's club meets the same night as the Lutheran women's club. If the Lutherans have a better speaker, some of our ladies slip over there. Of course it works the other way too. One night I dropped in on a human relations meeting in my own church to see if I could round up a few volunteers for another parish project. Out of the first twenty I asked, I found eight Presbyterians, three Methodists, two Episcopalians, a Quaker, a Unitarian, a Jew and a Buddhist."

"Did you sign up any volunteers?"

"It took me a while, but I finally got the project going after the Quaker and the Unitarian caucused and elected the Buddhist lady chairman."

Monsignor O'Pshaw told me the sisters who staffed the parish school were being visited by their Mother General. So I went directly to the convent to speak to her. Sister M. Cassandra foresees a crisis in Catholic education.

"The problem of finding enough nuns to staff the schools is getting worse all the time. We keep hiring more and more lay teachers. The first thing they do is call a strike, so we have to pay them higher and higher salaries.

"We decided to research the problem. We fed all the trends on population, teacher availability, income and the like into a computer. We hoped the computer could give us a long-range projection that would help us figure out where we're going."

"How did the projection come out?"

Sister Cassandra turned her face away. "By 1982 even the Mother General of our order will be a layman."

The information Sister Cassandra gave me on the shortage of nuns suggested an investigation of the vocation situation. I went to Father Diogenes Smith, vocation director of the Stentorians, an order specializing in preaching and mass communications.

Father Diogenes told me the Stentorians face extinction. Only a few years ago they had two hundred in their novitiate. The total has shrunk to eight. The Stentorians have sold the novitiate and its grounds to the Hilton hotel chain and enrolled their eight young men at Harvard.

"Eight novices a year aren't enough to maintain the order," he complained. "Don't tell anyone, but we have more than eight marriages a year. As a Stentorian, I know how it felt to be the last of the passenger pigeons."

Father Diogenes said the order had tried everything to attract more young men, from national advertising to door-to-door calls. He plans to experiment with unorthodox methods. When I left his office, I saw two shifty-eyed men in the waiting room with a bloodhound on a long leash. I didn't have a chance to find out who they were.

My next call was on the well-known liturgical expert, Father John Ringling De Mille. I asked him to bring me up to date on changes in the form of worship. He excused himself from a rock-and-roll combo he had been auditioning and sat down with me.

"You have to understand that different facets of worship are emphasized at various periods according to the culture of the times. In the beginning it seems to have been something like a family meal. In recent times it has become theatrical, like opera. Most of what went on was in a language nobody understood. But since it was set to music, you couldn't have caught the words anyway. When the music was good, it was

still an emotional experience. Unfortunately, in most of the
outlying churches the music was awful.

"Now it's no longer thought of as a show. It's more of a
gathering—not easy-going like a family picnic, but still rather
formal like a company party when the boss's wife belongs to
the WCTU."

I asked Father De Mille if he didn't think the change of
emphasis from performance to participation was encouraging.
Although he's in favor of more participation by the people,
he's disturbed by their behavior.

"They get more informal every day. Next they'll be coming
to church in sports clothes, playing banjos and eating sandwiches."

"Do you think we'll lose the liturgical cycle?"

"No. They'll probably go symbolic with the sandwiches—
kosher corned beef during Advent, liver sausage in Lent, egg
salad at Easter."

"I can understand the other two, but why liver sausage for
Lent?"

"I don't like liver sausage."

I said I thought more informality would attract people, especially the young, to worship, perhaps offsetting the effects of
the alarming trends I had been hearing about. Father De Mille
disagreed.

"That might be true for a while," he said. "But they'd start
dropping off before long. How much liver sausage can a person
stand?"

At this point in my quest, I decided I had heard enough of
pastoral and sociological considerations. It was time to dig
down to the essence of truth by interviewing a professional
theologian. I was assured by several sources that the best man
to talk to was Father Gloom of Armageddon College. Having
been fired at Catholic University early in his career, Father
Gloom naturally has become one of the most widely respected
theologians in the country.

I cornered Father Gloom just after he had finished a lecture in which he predicted that the Church, which was once entirely contained within a small upper room, will eventually shrink back to that size. When I insisted, he explained how he had reached such a somber conclusion.

"To start, there are about half-a-billion Catholics in the world. You can add to this all the other Christians and Christian fellow-travelers, but to be honest about it you'd have to subtract all those who were baptized and then never gave religion another thought. On this exchange I doubt that you'd come out even.

"Then, a third of all the Catholics in the world are in Latin America, where Christianity is a thin veneer on top of pre-Columbian Indian religion. Not really a dynamic force. If they can solve their economic problems, those people will go secularist as surely as 'Coca-Cola' in Spanish is still 'Coca-Cola.' If they can't straighten out their economy and their politics, the Communists will get them. *Adios* to nearly two hundred million.

"In Asia, the Chinese sooner or later will brainwash everybody. Gone: forty million more. In Africa, the rise of nationalism and the identification of Christianity with nineteenth-century colonialism will cost us that continent, along with more than twenty million Catholics.

"In Europe, more than two hundred forty million Catholics are trapped between Dutch theologians and the Spanish and Italian hierarchies. Obviously, there isn't much hope for these unfortunate people. We're guaranteed always to have a Pope, of course, even if he's the last bishop on earth. But he'll never be able to stay in Europe.

"That brings us to North America, where Canadian Catholics are French and Mexican Catholics are Spanish, hence likely to go down the drain with France and Spain. That leaves in all the world only the United States. And although we have more than forty million Catholics, those west of the Mississippi are

too conservative to move with the times and those east of the
Mississippi are already boiling over with heretical notions."
   I exclaimed, "You've written off absolutely everybody!"
   "Not everybody. There remain the Pope, and you, and I."
Father Gloom looked at me disapprovingly. "But I must say I
have my doubts about you."
   This remark offended me. I had no desire to spend any time
in an upper room with Father Gloom, so I left at once without
waiting for the end of the world.

Peace—With or Without Pot

TRUDGEON & BLUDGEON
ATTORNEYS
14 East Elm Street, Newburg, Illinois

Most Rev. Henry Clearworthy
Bishop of Newburg
1234 Main St.
Newburg, Ill.

Your Excellency:
   With all the talk about collegiality and lay responsibility in
the Church nowadays, I feel I should bring to your attention
a situation that has arisen in my home parish, St. Savonarola.
Although as a loyal son of the Church I have accepted all of
the disturbing changes resulting from the Council in an obedient
spirit, I consider the haste to make changes at St. Savonarola
quite unseemly. We are always the first to try anything new.
   Sunday was the last straw. I arrived for nine o'clock mass as
usual, sat in my usual place—and thought I was in the wrong
church. Instead of our fine organ (for which I helped raise
$14,000 not long ago), up in the choir loft they began playing

the weirdest collection of instruments imaginable. I recognized guitars, horns and DRUMS!

I couldn't believe anything so worldly and inappropriate to worship could be allowed in a Catholic church. If Your Excellency has authorized music of this sort, I shall have to accept it as I have all the other changes; but I strongly suspect this particular experiment was conducted without your approval or knowledge.

This would be in keeping with the general atmosphere of restlessness, seeking after novelty and disrespect for traditional values so prevalent today—especially in this parish.

Sincerely yours,
J. WILLIAM TRUDGEON

DIOCESE OF NEWBURG
1234 Main Street, Newburg, Illinois

Mr. J. William Trudgeon
Trudgeon & Bludgeon
14 E. Elm St.
Newburg, Ill.

Dear Mr. Trudgeon:

Under instructions from His Excellency, Bishop Clearworthy, I wish to acknowledge your recent letter. His Excellency read your communication with great interest and asked me to thank you for it in his name.

With every good wish, I am

Sincerely yours,
REV. TIMOTHY O'BRIEN
Secretary to the Bishop

CENTER COLLEGE
DEPARTMENT OF HISTORY
Newburg, Illinois

Bishop Henry Clearworthy
Diocese of Newburg
1234 Main St.
Newburg, Ill.

Dear Bishop Clearworthy:

No disrespect to your office or to your person is intended by this letter; however, in the spirit of Vatican II, my conscience impels me to advise you that your recent decision to prohibit priests from participating in the anti-war smoke-in demonstration may prove to be a serious mistake in the eyes of history.

I myself do not approve of the vast amount of marihuana being smoked by the students on campus here, but the dangers of marihuana seem to have been overexaggerated, and I don't believe the Church can afford to stand aloof from involvement with young people in the areas of life where their interests lie.

Furthermore, the purpose of the smoke-in is to demonstrate against war, a highly moral purpose which should enjoy the support of the Church rather than its condemnation. After all, to demonstrate solidarity on this issue it will not be necessary for the priests actually to smoke any marihuana themselves. Their physical presence alone would help the Church make a statement on the immorality and wickedness of the war policy.

I sincerely hope you may yet find your way clear to refine your position and permit the priests to march under the same figurative banner I myself support: "Peace—With or Without Pot."

Sincerely,
JAMES KEEN
Assistant Professor

DIOCESE OF NEWBURG
1234 Main Street, Newburg, Illinois

Mr. James Keen
Assistant Professor
Department of History
Center College
Newburg, Ill.

Dear Mr. Keen:
Under instructions from His Excellency, Bishop Clearworthy, I wish to acknowledge your recent letter. His Excellency read your communication with great interest and asked me to thank you for it in his name.
With every good wish, I am

Sincerely yours,
Rev. Timothy O'Brien
Secretary to the Bishop

THE PINES
Sunrise Ridge Road, Box 14 Route 3, Newburg, Illinois

Most Rev. Henry Clearworthy
Bishop of Newburg
1234 Main St.
Newburg, Ill.

Your Excellency:
Beware! There are forces at work in this diocese seeking to topple not only the American way of life but Holy Mother Church as well. They are watching me even now, so I hasten to warn you before it is too late.
They have agents in the rectories!!!
I have been going to daily Mass for many years. Suddenly I noticed they were wearing new vestments, and no matter what the color of day—green for the season, black for funerals or

whatever—there is always a touch of RED somewhere in the design. That's their secret sign. One of the curates even has a red car.

Save us before it's too late. Please, please don't tell anybody I was the one who gave them away.

Obediently yours,
MATILDA PEARSON

Miss Matilda Pearson
The Pines
Sunrise Ridge Road
Box 14 Route 3
Newburg, Ill.

Dear Miss Pearson:
Under instructions from His Excellency, Bishop Clearworthy, I wish to acknowledge your recent letter. His Excellency read your communication with great interest and asked me to thank you for it in his name.

With every good wish, I am

Sincerely yours,
REV. TIMOTHY O'BRIEN
Secretary to the Bishop

NEWBURG FURNITURE CO.
11 Main Street, Newburg, Illinois

Most Rev. Henry Clearworthy
Bishop of Newburg
1234 Main St.
Newburg, Ill.

Your Excellency:
According to our records, the Diocese purchased a chair last February (Catalog No. 175684, beige) priced at $254.19, in-

cluding tax and discount. Despite our rendering several bills and contacting your accounting department several times, we still have not received payment.

If there is some objection about the merchandise or our service, we would be happy to discuss the problem with you, but no such complaint has been received.

I am hoping you will be able to look into this matter and expedite payment.

Cordially yours,
ROBERT NELSON
Credit Manager

DIOCESE OF NEWBURG
1234 Main Street, Newburg, Illinois

Mr. Robert Nelson
Credit Manager
Newburg Furniture Co.
11 Main St.
Newburg, Ill.

Dear Mr. Nelson:

Under instructions from His Excellency, Bishop Clearworthy, I wish to acknowledge your recent letter. His Excellency read your communication with great interest and asked me to thank you for it in his name.

With every good wish, I am

Sincerely yours,
REV. TIMOTHY O'BRIEN
Secretary to the Bishop

P.S. The chair was never delivered.

T.O'B.

BAR X RANCH
Cataract, Colorado,
Jim Sturgis, Prop.

Most Rev. Henry Clearworthy
Bishop of Newburg
1234 Main St.
Newburg, Ill.

Dear Hank:

Are you coming in July or not? We're starting to fill up, and if you don't let me know soon, all of our guest rooms will be gone. Of course, you're always welcome to squeeze in somewhere, but you won't get the kind of rest you need bunking with the hands.

Remember Al Blake? He was here last week. He's president of a bank in Denver now. I told him he'd done well for someone Sister Emelda always said was the naughtiest kid in seventh grade. He said he was only the second naughtiest kid in seventh grade; you were the worst.

He was full of up-to-date news about the old gang. Too much to write. I'll tell you all when you get here.

Best,
Jim

DIOCESE OF NEWBURG
1234 Main Street, Newburg, Illinois

Mr. James Sturgis
Bar X Ranch
Cataract, Colorado

Dear Mr. Sturgis:

Under instructions from His Excellency, Bishop Clearworthy, I wish to acknowledge your recent letter. His Excellency read your communication with great interest and asked me to thank you for it in his name.

With every good wish, I am

Sincerely yours,
REV. TIMOTHY O'BRIEN
Secretary to the Bishop

BAR X RANCH
Cataract, Colorado
Jim Sturgis, Prop.

Most Rev. Henry Clearworthy
Bishop of Newburg
1234 Main St.
Newburg, Ill.

Dear Hank:
You lowdown coyote. What's the idea of sending *me* a form letter? You're cracking up. Or else you've been riding your staff so hard that *they're* cracking up. In either case you need a rest from each other. I'm definitely reserving that room for you in July.

Best,
JIM

BISHOP'S RESIDENCE
923 Washington Drive, Newburg, Illinois

Mr. Jim Sturgis
Bar X Ranch
Cataract, Colorado

Dear Jim:
You're right about my needing a rest. I'm looking forward to seeing you and Helen in July as planned.

Sorry about the form letter. You wouldn't believe the volume of mail we've been getting since the Council. Even using form letters, we get behind and make mistakes. In the future, you'd better write me here on Washington Drive instead of at the office.

I'm hopeful that our system will soon improve. We're having a consultant come in and streamline our procedures, so we can handle mail more efficiently, the way they do in business.

Yore pard,
HANK

NEWBURG FURNITURE CO.
11 Main Street, Newburg, Illinois

Dear Customer:

This card is to acknowledge your recent complaint. Our president has read your communication with great interest. We are investigating the matter and hope to give you a satisfactory answer as soon as possible.

NEWBURG FURNITURE CO.

Remember to Keep Your Wedding Garment Handy

The Spanish hierarchy has approved new rules for clerical attire. Spanish priests are still expected to wear cassocks in public. Off duty, they may wear a clerical suit with Roman collar whenever "reasonable." To wear civilian clothes requires written permission of a superior officer in each case.

This sounds rather like the uniform rules that used to be in effect in the U. S. Armed Forces. Authorities issued orders for a "uniform of the day," sometimes forgetting to look at the weather forecast first. The Navy issued me a warm, comfortable turtleneck sweater then reproved me for wearing it under my fatigue shirt during a cold snap because it wasn't part of the uniform of the day. In Spain the cassock is simply the uniform of the day every day.

The cassock does have its advantages. As with the Scotsman's kilt, you can't tell what is being worn underneath it. My priest friends have brought me to suspect that under most cassocks are loud sport shirts that would give a bat the blind staggers. Concealing these shirts from view, the cassock performs a valuable public service.

This uniform-of-the-day concept suggests to me that it might be a good idea to spell out the appropriate garb for religious on various occasions. For instance, there should be some sort of riot suit for priests and nuns to wear while taking part in civil-rights demonstrations. It ought to include a safety helmet similar to that worn by a construction worker or a miner. Then, if rocks are thrown at the demonstrators, injuries will be fewer.

The reversible jacket suggests several possibilities. One side could be black leather for wearing in the inner-city apostolate while the other would be a soft garment, appropriate when the wearer is transferred to an assignment in a middle-class suburb.

I have always wished monsignors would wear oak leaves or eagles on their lapels so I could tell the very reverends from the right reverends. Like stalactites versus stalagmites, this is something I never have been able to keep straight.

For laymen, the practice of wearing special clothes on Sunday should be revived. Years ago, most people wore the rough work clothes of the farmer or the mechanic all week, dressing up only on Sunday for church. In small towns there was nowhere else to go. Nowadays, of course, many men wear the same kind of clothes almost all the time—to work, to parties, to church. How drab! Yet, no one would think of playing golf in a hunting jacket or wearing a boating cap to the bowling alley.

Women have maintained a consciousness of levels of dress.

They distinguish infinite gradations of formality ranging down-
ward from the evening gown to the cocktail dress to the tailored
suit to the housedress. At the very bottom of the scale is the
dressing gown, clutched about the wearer with one hand while
the other hand brews the coffee and loosens the curlers. But
women, too, have fallen away from thinking of "Sunday best."

The problem of designing special clothes to wear to church can
be approached in various ways. A utilitarian outfit might include a built-in change-maker for dealing with multiple collections. And a couple of large, strong loops sewed onto the side
of the jacket would make it easier to pack home the Sunday
paper.

A liturgical costume for men might include neckties that
matched the color of the priest's vestments and concealed the
wires of a headphone set. Like airliners with their choice of
sound channels for each passenger—TV, popular or classical
music—pews could be wired for sound. Each member of the congregation could plug into the type of accompaniment he pre-
ferred—organ or guitar—for hymn singing. And no one else would
be distracted.

The ecumenical uniform would require padded knees. When
a Protestant visits a Catholic church, the first thing he notices
that makes him feel strange is the kneeling boards. Most
Protestant churches do not have them. If the Catholics began
coming to church with padded knees, the kneelers could be
taken out, resulting in both a friendly interfaith gesture and
elimination of a substantial expense from church budgets.

A friend of mine who is big in ecclesiastical goods has been
running some surveys around the country to see how he might
cash in on the new market in special clothes for religious and
quasi-religious occasions. One idea he tested—a suit with a padded seat for sitting through graduation and cornerstone-laying
ceremonies—was vetoed by survey respondents as offensive to
pious—ah—ears. More acceptable were waterproof vests and
sleeves for godparents at baptisms, sheepskin coats for parishioners who like to think of themselves as part of the pastor's flock

and easily removable shirts to wear during large-scale fund drives.

These shirts have two layers. In the outer layer is a special pocket for the money with your name and address embroidered on it. With a flip of the zipper, the outer layer detaches. It lets you give the shirt off your back, and nobody can say you didn't.

Amid today's currents of change, it is difficult to predict how decisions on such matters may be reached. As in the past, an order could be handed down through a committee of Italian cardinals. And the results might be good, especially if their eminences were in touch with the sharp new Italian fashions through a couple of nephews in the business. Much as one might prefer the collegial method, certain hazards exist in putting such a question to a vote at the grass roots. Some incompletely assimilated ethnic parishes would want to see everyone in white satin with purple trimmings.

A benefit to be derived from more diversified clothing could be the singling out of various members of the congregation so that their good example would be noted and emulated. Those who attend mass every Sunday and support the parish would be entitled to wear silver buttons on their church suits. If they also read the Catholic press, engaged in apostolic works and formed right consciences on social issues, they would get to wear gold buttons. Any layman wealthy and generous enough to endow a professorship at a Catholic college would receive a seamless robe. After a gift like that he wouldn't need pockets any more.

Humbug, Humbug, Fly Away Home

Most people agreed years ago that Christmas is no longer a Christian holiday. The question has become not *whether* we should be doing something different but *what.*

I have watched many families struggle with this problem, including my friends, Donald and Gay Apparel. They decided they didn't want their small children confusing Santa Claus with Christ, so they moved the sock-hanging bit ahead to December 6, the feast of St. Nicholas. This was supposed to make December 25 a day of more religious significance.

But the neighbors didn't understand. Don and Gay were referred to in the neighborhood as "Mr. and Mrs. Scrooge," the couple who were telling all the little children that there wasn't any Santa Claus.

At the Apparel house the children hung their stockings on December 6 and received some inexpensive trinkets and treats. The main gifts were reserved for Christmas Day. "In other words," said Don Apparel a few years later when the custom had become a family ritual impervious to change, "we now have two materialistic Christmases, a little one and a big one."

When a formal movement to "put Christ back into Christmas" began gathering momentum several years ago, I was delighted. After it had achieved some success, I wasn't so sure it was a good idea. First, I had to concede that when non-Christian citizens and taxpayers objected to the display of Christian symbols on public property, often at public expense, they had a point. Christmastime seems an especially poor season to ram peace and good will down the neighbors' throats whether they like it or not.

Then, when the commercial interests started to go along with the campaign, I was appalled on esthetic grounds. In the old days, the department stores filled their windows with elves and reindeer and merchandise—unabashedly taking advantage of a prime selling season. Now, many stores set aside one window for a Nativity scene. The other windows, of course, are still full of elves and reindeer and merchandise. It jolts me to see the Holy Family tucked in between the elves and the electric toothbrushes, almost as if they were endorsing the goods on display.

And how do you explain to the children that the plaster elves in one window are purely legendary while the plaster crèche in the next window is a representation of the central event of history?

I thought for a while that my reaction was a personal peculiarity. Then I met a charming and intelligent young nun who is an expert on the psychology of preschool children. She argued that the crèche (which was invented by St. Francis of Assisi in 1223) is confusing to young children, not only in department store windows, but anywhere. Just about the time a young child begins to form an image of God as a loving father-figure, she said, along comes Christmas and there's God all of a sudden a baby lying in a manger.

Christmas charity is another problem. One year Don and Gay Apparel decided to reduce their spending on gifts to their children and relatives in order to send the difference to charity, which seems a Christian thing to do at Christmas. But by the following December, Donald Junior had been promised a new bicycle so he could have a paper route, young Holly was on the list for quite a few new clothes (which, in point of fact, she needed) and the other children had filed requests which Don and Gay could not ignore without discriminating unfairly. However, Don's income was no larger. When Don reviewed the figures at income tax time, he was chagrined to discover that the Christmas alms were actually subtracted, not from the gift budget, as intended, but from the other charitable contributions the family customarily made throughout the year. "We robbed both Peter and Paul," he explained.

Don and Gay also have been brooding about the prevalence of impersonal, institutionalized charity in our society. Gay likes the idea of the traditional Christmas basket, despite its overtones of paternalism, because it gives the giver a chance to help a particular person with a smile and a friendly word as well as a material gift.

The first Christmas the Apparels tried it, their advance

Christmas basket information proved inaccurate. Along with the food, they dropped off a load of dolls for a large family that seemed to run mostly to boys. The next Christmas their basket family moved out of town on Christmas Eve, leaving the Apparels with an extra defrosted turkey to dispose of on Christmas Day. Trying to give away a turkey on Christmas Day is like trying to sell last year's calendar—worse, actually, because everybody hasn't just eaten a calendar.

Last Christmas Don and Gay went out once more with a Christmas basket. They lugged it up the stairs and knocked on the door. An elderly gentleman opened it a crack and said: "Too late. You'll have to take that junk somewhere else. The elves were here this morning and filled my shoes with gold."

Not only don't we know what to do on Christmas, we can't even agree on a definition of the Christmas season. Millions who are engaged in the manufacture and distribution of consumer goods observe Christmas at work in midsummer. Retail stores start the season the week before Thanksgiving. In past years, while most of the country was already wassailing and singing carols, Don and Gay have observed an austere Advent, permitting themselves no more than a couple of verses of "O Come, O Come, Emanuel."

When, according to the liturgy, the Christmas season actually began, the Apparels tried on occasion to give a rollicking caroling party. It was always a flop. Their friends, irascible with chronic mild hangovers, couldn't be persuaded to sing. "If I hear one more 'fa-la-la-la-la,' I'll scream," said one. "I'm looking forward to Lent."

Like other families, Don and Gay haven't given up. With courage and good will, they set out anew each year to keep Christmas, ever hoping to grope their way to a form of celebration that will prove both rational and appropriate. The perseverance of so many in their search can itself be taken as an example of the true Christmas spirit. Right, Virginia?

Is This On or Off the Record,
Mr. Groundhog?

The advent of Groundhog Day always sets me to meditating about the destiny of the press. Since the newspapers never fail to interview Mr. Groundhog on February 2 and report whether he sees his shadow, Groundhog Day is an appropriate symbol of the concern of the press with trivia. Also, Groundhog Day kicks off the observance of Catholic Press Month. While the Catholic press has not wasted space on Mr. Groundhog, it has many a Marmota Monax of its own (that's Latin for groundhog).

The Catholic press used to point a finger at the secular press and complain about its sensationalism and bias. Only in the Catholic press, it was claimed, could the reader get the truth. Sometimes this was the fact, sometimes not. The paradox was that the secular press cherished a higher ideal of service than the Catholic press did.

For all its lapses, the secular press held ideals to which reporters and editors generally subscribed. We felt uncomfortable when the code wasn't observed. Moreover, staff members were trained to a professional response that usually made the code operate automatically.

When Mayor Groundhog said Alderman Possum was really a skunk, the paper routinely contacted Alderman Possum before writing the story so that charge and countercharge, if any, could be presented at the same time. A paper that wouldn't give Alderman Possum his say because its publisher supported Mayor Groundhog tended to lose its best staff members.

Some of the main points of the code could be stated as follows:

1. A newspaper's highest duty is to publish the news the citizens need in order to play a responsible role in a free society.

2. This requires keeping the spotlight of publicity on the authorities whose decisions affect the general welfare.

3. The truth must never be suppressed because some VIP who could make trouble for the paper or its staff might be offended.

4. In controversies, all parties are entitled to a fair presentation of their views—even when the paper disagrees with them.

Just as the secular press sometimes failed to observe this code, the Catholic press sometimes rose above the limitations it set for itself. But the typical Catholic publication of years ago thought it ought to be more like an industry house organ than an independent newspaper. The code it followed could be worded like this:

1. A Catholic newspaper's highest duty is to publish news that presents the Church to its members in a favorable light.

2. This requires keeping the spotlight of publicity away from authorities on occasion (everybody makes mistakes).

3. The truth may be suppressed when it might scandalize the little ones.

4. In controversies, some arguments may be ignored because error has no rights.

Even before Vatican II, the Catholic press was growing beyond this position, and since the Council the rate of change has speeded up. The code now would have to read something like this:

1. A Catholic newspaper's highest duty is to publish the news the Catholic community needs to participate fully as responsible members of the Church and Christians in society.

2. This requires keeping the spotlight of publicity on authorities because their actions can't help affecting the responsibilities of the man in the pew.

3. The truth must never be suppressed because that's the greatest scandal of all.

4. In controversies, all persons are entitled to fair treatment because they are persons.

Understandably, many Catholics, both clerical and lay, haven't quite got used to the new approach. If asked, they probably would agree wholeheartedly with the principles. But when the code begins to operate day to day, they find it unsettling.

Let us suppose Father Badger, a vigorous young priest, makes rather a nuisance of himself leading demonstrations against the new beaver dam. He claims it is an immoral infringement on the rights of the poor, whose homes will be flooded. Bishop Possum is under considerable pressure. The Beavers, who are important community leaders, say the dam is needed to benefit everyone. They want the bishop to silence Father Badger, whose support consists mainly of a mass of miserable and inarticulate Muskrats.

Seeking a middle course in a complex situation, Bishop Possum refuses to order Father Badger to desist but he does transfer him to another parish where there aren't any Muskrats. Years ago, the whole affair could have been handled quietly behind the scenes, and neither Catholic nor secular press would have intervened.

Nowadays, the story inevitably comes to the attention of Catholic Editor Fox, who has been professionally trained in journalism and automatically makes a professional response. Father Badger and Bishop Possum are interviewed. Statements are acquired from the chief Beavers. Sample opinions are collected to represent the Muskrat in the street (or creek). A factual account of the results is published under a headline like this:

BISHOP POSSUM TRANSFERS

FATHER BADGER IN DISPUTE

OVER FLOODING MUSKRAT HOMES

Some readers, not yet accustomed to the new ways, mis-
understand. Bishop Possum thinks Fox is criticizing him and
trying to undermine his authority because the story includes
unkind comments about the bishop that are circulating in the
Muskrat neighborhood. A couple of Beavers complain that the
whole controversy over the dam is Fox's fault because if he
hadn't printed anything, the affair might have blown over.

Fox's defense is that there is no escape from confronting the
moral question raised by the dam. Is Father Badger right in
his opposition? Does Bishop Possum consider the dam moral?
If not, why is he transferring Father Badger? Fox does not know
all the answers. But he can print the facts as they emerge so
that answers can be found.

One day a pack of Squirrels, who have no interest in the dam
but don't like Muskrats, catch Father Badger and toss him into
the creek. Secular magazines and television come running. A
Catholic national magazine appears with a profile article on
Father Badger and his photo on the cover, whiskers still drip-
ping.

"Why is the Catholic press picking on our diocese?" asks
the venerable Groundhog, noted both for his lifelong friendship
with Bishop Possum and his generous support of charitable
institutions.

It is not easy to explain that the new spirit of honesty encouraged in the Church by the Council is simply being reflected in the Catholic press. The community is jolted by the
impact resulting from the combination of new goals and professional methods. That's how the fur flies.

The Age of Renewals

A friend of mine has prescient dreams. He says they're in full color with wide screen and original musical score. I never paid any attention until he forecast the progressive turn of the Vatican Council at a time when no one else in our circle would have dreamed it was possible. Now I listen to him.

Recently, he dreamed about the Catholic press. This is a term that refers to a few magazines and newspapers that are deserving but poor and a great many other magazines that are both poor and undeserving. In my friend's dream, he found himself looking backward from some future time—the very year in which a leading Catholic magazine surpassed *Reader's Digest* in circulation.

He further dreamed that Catholic publications generally were enjoying zooming circulations and lush advertising revenues. The most important papers had organized an international news service with nearly as many fulltime correspondents as the leading secular wire service, and far more editorial enterprise.

There had been quite a scandal when CPI (Catholic Press International) was discovered to have bugged the Vatican as thoroughly as if it were the American Embassy in Moscow. Most outrageous of all was the disclosure of a CPI microphone hidden in the Pope's ring.

The Executive Editor of CPI brazened out the affair. "Some of our younger men were a bit overzealous," he conceded, "but, thanks to CPI, Catholics nowadays can't say they don't know what's going on in the Church."

"Are you going to discipline the staff members responsible?" he was asked.

"No, I think they've suffered enough. The men on that job had to work in shifts with earphones on, listening to the signals from the miniature mike in the ring. They did pick up some hot news leads, but there was considerable ring-kissing. And 'smack, smack, smack' all day long gets to be a grind."

The Catholic papers were able to afford a variety of syndicated features which, in the old days, had been limited to the secular press. Although there was no horoscope, nothing else was missing. The new crossword puzzles aimed right at the readership. Number 17 down, four letters beginning with K, "a liberal theologian of the mid-sixties."

On the comic pages some remarkable transformations had occurred as the top strips followed the top dollar. Orphan Annie, after attending a school staffed by fiery young sisters, was now not only a lady but an intellectual as well. Even Daddy Warbucks admitted to entertaining more advanced social thought.

The most successful magazine in the country was *Diaspora*, edited especially for millionaires named Kennedy. There were twenty million of them—or at least it seemed like it—and they all subscribed to *Diaspora*. Since even a few non-Kennedys also subscribed, its circulation was enormous.

The Catholic press was now highly sophisticated in audience selectivity, making the special interest magazines and regional editions of the 1960s seem crude and primitive. An advertiser could buy circulation not only market by market but parish by parish, in magazines that distinguished among all the various shades of opinion on such topics as liturgical reform and birth control.

Pray and Sway delivered eighty-three per cent of all the far-out liturgy enthusiasts in the country. Manufacturers of all kinds of products with appeal to the younger set (especially guitars) had to wait for a turn to busy advertising space.

For families that stood by the traditional position on family limitation, viewing even rhythm with a certain distaste, the leading magazine was *Family Way*. Its space salesmen stressed the fact that *Family Way's* readership averaged 9.3 children per household and comprised a lucrative market for encyclopedias, children's clothes, food products and similar items.

The most conservative Catholic readership went to *Crusade*. The editorial policy of *Crusade* was simple and consistent. *Crusade* was against things: especially dirty movies, dirty books, dirty dirt and the United Nations.

These were the leading magazines according to advertising revenue. A few other magazines, with less cabin cruiser advertising, nevertheless enjoyed substantial circulations and prestige. The most liberal was *Church Militant*, the combined voice of three important unions—the Priest's Guild, the United Brothers and the International Brotherhood of Sisters, C.I.O. Equally influential on the conservative side was the weekly newsletter of the hierarchy, *Changing Epochs*.

There was even a monthly for altarboys called *Prayboy*.

With so much money on their hands because of their success, Catholic publishers were following the same pattern as the secular publishers of years before. They were branching out into other communications media. There was scarcely an important diocese or publisher anywhere that did not own television and radio stations and film studios as well as publishing enterprises.

The general public's heightened interest in Catholic affairs shattered old concepts of television programming. Where once *Bonanza* had led the ratings, the top show now was *Plethora*, the heart-warming true-life story of a middle-aged layman who'd had it up to *here* with worthy cause fund appeals (because he still had 9.3 children to send to college).

Influential figures in the Church had become used to working with the mass media. They now realized that being misquoted on the late newscast was not a sign that the gates of Hell were about to prevail. In fact, most could even bear to be quoted accurately in prime time. However, there was still Heaven to pay around the chancery office on Monday morning after the bishop's series of talking pastoral letters bombed out in the ratings.

At this point in my friend's account of his dream, I interrupted him. I accused him of laying it on too thick. My friend said he'd had more than one dream about the Catholic press. Sometimes it all happened another way.

"As in Dickens," he said, "The Ghost of Christmases That Might Have Been But For the Week That Was—or however that story goes. I forget exactly."

In another of his dreams, the Catholic press had virtually gone under. First, the secular press became so interested in Catholic news that their coverage was just as extensive as that of the Catholic press, and even more timely. Second, secular media became more willing than ever to publish Catholic writers and present Catholic viewpoints. Third, the various religious orders and dioceses that had been subsidizing unprofitable periodicals found that they needed their money for other enterprises.

The Catholic Press Association (which I remember meeting in plush hotels like the Waldorf) thereafter held its conventions in a sixth-grade classroom of a parish school somewhere in Kansas to be near the geographical center of the country and save travel expenses.

"Stop, stop!" I shouted, like Scrooge. "It's too horrible. Is there no other way?"

My friend said he'd sleep on it.

Inside the Outside

For many years there has been a tradition that Catholic institutions must operate as mirror images of secular ones. If there is an American Gyrokinetics Society, there has to be an American Catholic Gyrokinetics Society. When AGS zigs,

ACGS zags. ACGS will eventually get around to zigging, too, but not before there has been a zag lag of a few years.

Similarly, there have always been the Catholic equivalents of various secular publications and their features, right down to Catholic comic strips. But it could be worse. Some features of the secular press have not been copied, at least not yet. You may be more grateful if I mention some of the types of columns you have been saved from till now.

For instance, the Catholic press could have had another Washington column. If all the copy written each day by Washington correspondents, counting the representatives of trade journals and magazines as well as daily newspapers and wire services, were stacked up, the pile would reach exactly to the top of the Washington Monument. This is verified from time to time by the Bureau of Standards. Whenever the stack is higher than the monument, friendly congressmen dispose of the excess by having it inserted in the *Congressional Record*.

The most important Washington columns are the ones used as trial balloons by the government. Someone in the administration tips off a columnist that the President is considering making a deal with China. "We'll trade them Formosa for Boardwalk and Park Place with two houses on each and a free pass at GO." When the chosen columnist reports the news, a severe public reaction develops. The public wants more than one pass at GO. Having found out what it wanted to know, the administration can then denounce the idea.

A Catholic adaptation of the trial-balloon column would be embarrassing nowadays. I wouldn't want to write one. In many dioceses around the country almost anything may be leaked to the press. Judging from recent news, a bishop's private correspondence is rather more likely to get into the papers than most senators' speeches. I'd rather not know who's being transferred where and who's being picketed for what. It depresses me.

Advice to the lovelorn? I'm afraid this type of column will spread. Catholic publications have already set a precedent with question box columns that could turn into advice to the lovelorn overnight. All that's holding them back is the incredible complexity of so many of the questions.

"Dear Father: I recently married a woman who was previously divorced from a man who had been married trigamously to both her sisters by an unfrocked Tlinget medicine man while acting as captain of a park bench that floated out to sea when they forgot to turn off the lawn sprinklers. I have two questions—which marriage is valid and should I tithe ten per cent of her income before or after taxes?"

Few columnists are qualified to deal with questions like this. A Hollywood column could be written with a Catholic slant. I might try my hand at it myself since I have had some experience interviewing theatrical celebrities. Years ago when I was a newspaper reporter I had occasion to ask Loretta Young how she liked changing trains in Chicago when even a hog could ride straight through. She said she could stand it, considering the difference in accommodations.

Another time, the late Carmen Miranda told me the reason she avoided extremes in her night club and movie costumes. (I don't recall whether she was a Catholic, but she came from a Latin country.) She said she had an enormous appendectomy scar. I suppose this might be considered inside information of a sort—a scoop by Hollywood news standards—but she had such a charming personality I forgot to put it in my story.

I was on hand at the airport one morning when a plane landed with two celebrities who had publicly eloped the night before from Hollywood. One was an actress noted more for her skill with a mascara brush than for acting ability. The other was an actor who starred in the kind of movies that always include underwater shots of the hero wrestling with crocodiles, sharks or submarines. Both had been married a couple of hundred times before. The reporters and photographers at the airport tried to reconstruct the tangled relationships. As I recall, it worked out that he was his own mother-in-law and she was both his aunt and his niece as well as his second, third and fourth cousin by marriage. The newspapers

and Hollywood writers had a circus with this story. The two
protagonists, on the ground in Chicago, were rumpled, sleepy-
eyed and surly.

A Catholic Hollywood column could have followed the story
with as much color as the rest, then pointed out the moral: if
there were more celibacy in the world, this sort of thing wouldn't
happen.

I haven't seen much musical criticism in Catholic publications. There's a good reason for this. If a columnist wrote that
the Philharmonic stinks this season, readers would say:

1. A Catholic should not be uncharitable.

2. They already read about it in the daily paper.

3. How many of the musicians in the orchestra are Catholics?

Or if he narrowed his scope in order not to duplicate the
secular media, the columnist would find himself saying that
the singing in the parish last Sunday truly moved him—out of
the church, where they were starting the high mass, down to
the basement chapel, where there was less of it.

Many other types of column remain possibilities for the
Catholic press—how to mind your Catholic baby and your
Catholic investments, how to pencil your Catholic eyebrows,
how not to figure your horoscope (we don't believe in horo-
scopes), what to watch on television (nothing), what's going
on in sports (nothing important). But so far none of these has
succeeded in displacing the opinions of the priests who are
serving time on the papers until they're old enough to be given
a parish.

Catholic publications do run columns on books. I don't
think any of the Catholic reviewers commands quite as much
prestige as the leading secular critics. I would like to participate
in the development of a renaissance of Catholic literary criticism. Then, when I recommended my friends' books and they
recommended mine, it would pay off in noticeable traffic at the
bookstores—just like the big time. What keeps me from starting
a new improved book column is my timing. I never seem to

get around to reading the important books till two or three years after they're published. Come to think of it, I still haven't read Sappho, Pindar or Marcus Aurelius and their books have been out even longer than that.

I once wrote a do-it-yourself column for a newspaper. I was specially chosen from all the members of the staff because I was the one who had always lived in an apartment where anything that couldn't be fixed with a beer-can opener—our only tool—was immediately thrown out. When I wrote a column on how to build your own garage, the readers could be sure I had done copious research. I had to, because otherwise I wouldn't have had the slightest idea. For a time, I considered offering a Catholic do-it-yourself column to some of my editor friends, but I couldn't think of anything to write about once I got past an Advent wreath and a Gothic martin house.

In brooding over the subject of columns, I decided that secular and Catholic press alike are ready for a new kind of column that hasn't been mentioned yet. It would be the world's first column by someone who doesn't have inside information about anything—and admits it.

The Leaning Tower of Babel

(Following is an excerpt from A *History of the Church Since 1975*, published in 1995 by Martin Luther O'Shaugnessy, Professor of Church History at Consolidated Christian University.)

*   *   *

It was not inevitable that the ecumenical movements of the 1960s and 1970s would result in the final Big Merger. There still were enough hostility and suspicion on all sides to prevent progress, if they had been allowed to coalesce. Fortunately, in the merger committees the main battles were not fought on basic issues of doctrine. Typical was the case of the Protestant group that went along with every premerger compromise proposed until the time came to settle whether the choir should wear robes. This group argued that their choir robes were predestined to be worn—at least until the robes were paid for.

But even difficult questions like this could be settled, so the Protestants were able to collect themselves into one big body embracing all the members of the old National Council of Churches as well as those denominations which formerly had considered the National Council of Churches thoroughly infiltrated by Communists or Jesuits or both.

Meanwhile, progress continued in talks between Roman Catholics and Orthodox Christians. The ancient differences in doctrinal formulations were smoothed over. The question of whether priests should have wives and beards created little difficulty. The sticky issue was negotiating a new deal on running the tourist attractions in Jerusalem.

In time, the Orthodox Church found itself in the curious position of being simultaneously merged with the Roman Catholics and, through the National Council of Churches, with the Protestants.

"It's got so I can't tell which way I'm supposed to vote nowadays on a school-bus referendum," said the Orthodox man-in-the-street.

The dilemma was finally resolved by the Big Merger that occurred in 1980, bringing all American Christians together into one church. As we all know, this long-awaited miracle did not immediately resolve all the Church's problems of disunity.

To understand why some differences lingered, it will be helpful to review the history of the churches. For the Catholics, the principal problem was the gift by Charlemagne of a temporal estate. This was supposed to free the Church from domination by a temporal prince, but it didn't work out too well. During those few years when the Church wasn't dominated by the ruler of France or the Emperor, it was noticed that the Pope himself was a temporal prince.

As anyone knows who has hung around buttering up chief executives, making decisions is a tricky business. It is not always possible to recognize a wise decision afterward, let alone beforehand. In order to be decisive at moments of crisis, the executive has to convince himself that his instincts are always right. Then he can toss off decisions as required without developing ulcers. It is difficult to maintain the necessary equanimity when there's a lot of ill-informed rabble running around questioning the decisions.

By keeping the grimy hands of the rabble off the tiller of the Bark of Peter, Catholics constructed an admirably logical structure of authority and doctrine, often envied by its most vocal critics. However, a certain inflexibility crept in that gradually converted a desirable conservativism into a cultural lag of centuries. In the twentieth century they were still wearing Roman clothes and erecting medieval buildings.

The problem of the Orthodox Church was similar: too much association with temporal power, leading to fragmentation along national boundaries. But for an accident of geography, there might be a Patriarch of Monte Carlo presiding over the independent Orthodox Church of Monaco.

As for the Protestants, they upheld the principle of freedom of conscience at a time when others gave it short shrift. The corollary of their position was an invitation to start your own church whenever you disagreed with the rest of the congregation, an invitation that many took advantage of over the years. At Flyspeck, North Dakota, the Reverend Mr. Theodore J. Smelser for many years headed the world's smallest independent denomination. It had only half a member. His explanation for this was: "Half the time I think nobody but me understands the Gospel; the other half the time I wonder if I understand it myself."

With the Big Merger all these religious currents—sound approaches overlaid with abuses—did not disappear, but a curious shift occurred. Instead of each group automatically continuing to argue in behalf of its own tradition, people began to discover common sympathies that crossed denominational bounds. Certain Catholics found they felt more comfortable with certain Presbyterians or Episcopalians than with some other Catholics, and vice versa.

What developed out of this melange of traditions and ideas were two groups within the Church similar to political parties. At first they were quite numerous—like the splinter parties of European politics—but the practicalities of running a vast organization quickly forced them into a two-party system like that of the United States. The two parties became known as "Protholics" and "Catestants." Each party embraced a considerable spectrum of opinion, often conflicting. Despite much overlapping, real differences between the parties remained.

Most religious journalists were suspected of Catestant leanings, although their publishers were uniformly Protholic.

During the constitutional convention, the splinter parties canceled each other out and had little influence on the proceedings. The big issue was representation. Some of the smaller denominations insisted that their Christmas and Easter attendance be included in computations of voting strength. In the final compromise, the smaller denominations were allowed to count fifty extra points for every community where they owned a church instead of renting a hall, with a hundred extra points if the mortgage had been retired.

The polarization of Protholics and Catestants began with the first national election to select new archbishops. (Some of the former Protestants didn't much like the idea of having archbishops, but they were persuaded to go along in return for the abolishment of door-to-door doughnut selling by children from parochial schools.)

The Protholic candidate for National Presiding Archbishop in that first election was the Most Reverend Machiavelli Moore, Bishop of Nuthaven, California. Bishop Moore had distinguished himself as an adroit administrator in the years after the Second Vatican Council by turning over his entire diocese to committees of laymen. The laymen soon had affairs so tangled and mismanaged they had to beg the bishop to step in and rescue them. At least, this was the version put out by the Protholic National Press Office. Surprisingly, a great many former Protestants were among Bishop Moore's supporters. They seem to have had experience with lay committees.

The Catestants nominated J. Wellington Forthright, a one-time field representative for Protestants and Others United for Separation of Church and State. He had been an Other and a son and grandson of Other ministers. Again a paradox was noted. He was backed by a large bloc of Catestants with Catholic backgrounds who seemed determined to resist undue clerical influence in the new Church.

During the campaign, Bishop Moore attacked Church spending. He spoke movingly of all the Protestant ladies serving church suppers and all the little nuns saving string for so many years. Now with the Big Merger in effect, he said, there was so much excess real estate on everyone's hands that it was time for the Church to economize by reducing or eliminating non-essential services. As the first step, he urged the end of all religious broadcasting on radio and television that no one tunes in. He agreed to exempt any program able to show it pulled a higher rating than the test pattern.

Mr. Forthright's campaign was built around the need to get the Church moving again after the period when its energies had been mainly absorbed by the Big Merger. He offered a three-point program:

1. In any community where churches of formerly different denominations were clustered in the same neighborhood, underground tunnels would be built to connect them. This would encourage everyone to realize they were now worshiping "under one roof." The tunnels also would speed the ushers on their rounds with the collection plate.

2. A centralized computer installation would be constructed so that no member of any of the federated churches could escape supporting worthy causes by claiming "I gave last year" or "I gave at the office."

3. All church-affiliated schools, colleges, hospitals and other institutions would be grouped in one giant administrative unit, with one supergiant budget to be raised by installing means of persuasion at the grass-roots level. His campaign slogan was "a thumbscrew in every pew."

Bishop Moore was elected by a narrow margin.

From the beginning, the Protholics showed themselves to be more conservative than the Catestants. At first, the Protholics were captured by their most conservative wing, who favored some rather extreme positions. On baptism, for instance, they held out not only for total immersion but a minimum dunk of thirty seconds in water not to exceed sixty-eight degrees Fahrenheit. They said this would separate the truly committed from the lukewarm. They also supported a bishop's authority to censor all utterances and writings of a religious nature, including the text of ad-lib prayers. (Machinery for carrying out this part of their program was not specified.)

The rightist grip on the Protholic party slipped after the great pilgrimage scandal. The Protholics, with their interest in tradition, attempted to revive a number of features of early and medieval Christianity. One of these that caught on for a while was the pilgrimage—until the press revealed that most of the pilgrims tended to wind up at places like Acapulco and the Riviera, with the connivance of leading rightist Protholics who "coincidentally" owned travel agencies.

Somewhat discredited, the most conservative Protholics were forced to yield control to a more moderate faction, who were satisfied to press for a few basics, such as maintaining Sunday as the day of worship and refraining from distributing ALL the Church's assets to the poor.

The bulk of the Catestants actually agreed on most matters with the bulk of the Protholics, but the liberal wing of the Catestants made more noise and received more attention from the mass media than anyone else. Far-out Catestants advocated making the question of the validity of orders moot by ordaining every man, woman and child at once. They argued in

favor of premarital sex on the grounds that it was an expression of the human personality and old taboos against it
antedated modern birth-control methods. Their influence waned
when they went too far by reinterpreting the Ten Commandments in the light of modern conditions. The new version fit
on the head of a pin, from which the ten thousand angels
who formerly danced there had been evicted.

Somehow, the new Church managed to avoid extremes, but
much careful steering was required to keep it in the middle of
the road.

Archbishop Moore later ran for Pope. He was defeated by
a Brazilian, who mustered the Indian vote against him by pointing out that Moore had been an Arizona cowboy in his youth.
This was especially effective in South America, where there are
lots of Indians and everyone goes to see Hollywood movies.
Upon retiring from public life, Archbishop Moore delivered a
thought-provoking address in which he recalled that he had
always favored ecumenism and the Big Merger. However, he
added, during his years in office he had frequently yearned for
the days when if a heretic obstructed progress you could just
take him out and burn him instead of having to appoint him
your auxiliary.

How to Tell Whether You're With It
or Up Against It

In recent years, personality testing in government and industry
has toad-stooled. (This is a more precise term for a process
sometimes described as "mushrooming.") Instead of having to
go through the agony of sizing up each employee as a person,
executives can base their personnel decisions on his answers to
standard questions like "would you rather attend a baseball
game or a symphony concert?"

During one of my depressive phases at an advertising agency I used to work for, I allowed myself to be persuaded to visit a company that was looking for an advertising manager. During the discussion of the fringe benefits, they mentioned their policy of giving personality tests to all prospective employees. I immediately lost all interest in their insurance plan, retirement plan and reserved parking spaces. If they thought they had a test that could predict whether a man would make a good advertising manager, they were even sillier than the people I was trying to escape from. I would be interested, however, in the results of a personality test given to men who like to give personality tests.

The Church no doubt will take a fling at personality testing sometime in the course of *aggiornamento*. The Church is always victimized to some extent by the superstitions of the age. Just as we had to burn a certain number of witches before we could free ourselves from belief in witchcraft, we'll probably have to let personality testing run its course.

To speed up this process and help get it over with, I have written the following tests. They are intended to help members of the Church at various levels to determine for themselves whether, when faced with change, they are psychologically with it or up against it.

Personality Test for Laymen

1. You go to mass on Sunday and hear guitar music coming from the choir loft. What is your first impulse?

a. To rend your garments and plug your ears with bits of your farthingale?

b. To jump into the aisle and dance (assuming it's tiled or carpeted so there are no slivers to hurt your bare feet)?

2. Further changes in the liturgy are announced. Why do you grumble?

a. Because if Latin was good enough for the Holy Trinity to use in conversing among Themselves, it ought to be good enough for worldly modern man?

b. Because you doubt that the authorities will ever get around to giving us a swinging liturgy—something psychedelic and peppy?

3. You are sitting quietly in the pew when you realize the sermon is attacking racial injustice. How do you react?

a. By standing up, shouting, "Homeowners have rights, too," and throwing a rock at the nearest nun?

b. By standing up, shouting, "Black power," and throwing a rock at the nearest policeman?

4. Your parish announces the beginning of a fund drive.

a. Do you volunteer to run the roulette booth and the craps table?

b. Do you complain that the money ought to be given to a worthier cause—like CARP (the Committee Against Reactionary Prelates)?

5. Your pastor preaches a passionate sermon against "so-called intellectuals."

a. Do you refuse to renew your subscription to *Reader's Digest?*

b. Do you nail ninety-five theses to the church door?

6. At the height of a controversy the authorities dismiss a professor or an editor. What is your immediate conclusion?

a. That the man was secretly a heretic, probably Arian or Albigensian, and had finally been caught at it?

b. That the victim had received a special charism from the Holy Spirit and was being persecuted for it by the corrupt Establishment?

7. You find out that a priest has left his parish and married. What is your assumption?

a. That he was spending too much time with the ladies of the choir?

b. That he is a creative theologian whose main purpose in taking a wife was intellectual companionship?

8. You read about the decline in seminary enrollments. What explanation occurs to you first?

a. That today's young people are being spoiled rotten by getting convertibles to drive to high school?

b. That today's young people are all intensely committed, either to the Peace Corps or to the New Left?

9. At a bridge party you are told that the neighbors are sending little Johnny to the public school now. Why do you think his parents are doing this?

a. Because the good sisters, after much patient suffering, finally expelled the little brat?

b. Because Johnny's parents discovered that, with all the teachers brilliant and dedicated, with no shortages of space or equipment, and with a staff psychiatrist for every three children, everything is perfect in the public schools?

10. You pick up a newspaper and learn that plans to start another new Catholic publication have been announced.

a. Are you cheered by this evidence of the Church's intention to continue spreading the Gospel by such up-to-the-minute methods as letter-press printing?

b. Do you take to your bed with an upset stomach, complicated by swelling of the magazine rack, anemia of the wallet and overstimulation of the retina?

SCORING:

If more than half your answers are *a*'s—Somebody should tell you Pius IX isn't the Pope any more.

If more than half your answers are *b*'s—You must be some kind of Protestant, although most denominations wouldn't have you.

Personality Test for Priests

1. When a penitent comes to you in confession with an exceedingly complex problem, what do you tell him?

a. To offer it up?

b. To see a psychiatrist?

2. What is your approach when you counsel a parishioner?

a. As soon as he tells you what his problem is, do you tell him what he should do in no uncertain terms?

b. Do you make him work it out for himself, non-directively, no matter how hard he begs for your advice?

3. A red-faced parishioner stamps into the rectory with a complaint. How do you handle him?

a. Do you assume he's a paranoid troublemaker and get rid of him at once?

b. Do you assume he's a committed Christian who cares about the Church and listen at length to his paranoid mutterings while you try to figure out what's bothering him?

4. At a parish social event a layman challenges some statement you have just made. What do you suspect?

a. That he probably has no more than a fourth-grade education and is incapable of grasping the subject?

b. That he has a doctorate in theology from Louvain and is setting a trap for you?

5. How would you describe the people of your parish?

a. Stingy, worldly and rebellious?

b. Stupid, reactionary and passive?

6. Who is your bishop?

a. The Boss?

b. The Enemy?

7. When you take a day off, what do you usually do?

a. Play golf?

b. Get arrested?

8. How do you feel about celibacy?

a. Do you think priests are better off to avoid women, who have been notorious since antiquity as traps set for the unwary by Satan?

b. Do you think men and women in marriage ordinarily possess a serene mutual understanding of such profound spiritual depth that priests also ought to participate in this mature relationship?

9. How would you prefer that mass be said?

a. For as many people as possible, ideally in a church big enough to hold the entire parish at one mass?

b. For as few people as possible, ideally for one Christian at a time in his own closet?

10. What was the most important fact you as a pastor learned from becoming acquainted with the gang at the local ministerial association?

a. That the Protestant clergy has the same problems you have with interfering laymen?

b. That it would be desirable to swap your assistants for a couple of young divinity-school graduates if they'd throw in a good pitcher?

SCORING:

If more than half your answers are *a*'s—You may profit from becoming familiar with the next test.

If more than half your answers are *b*'s—You'd better go back and try the test for laymen.

Personality Test for Bishops

1. When you took over your diocese what did you do about existing diocesan officials?

a. Weeded them out to prevent them from sticking together and obstructing your time-tested policies?

b. Weeded them out because they probably harbored reactionary sympathies?

2. In general, how would you describe the priests of your diocese?

a. Dangerously liberal, rash and insubordinate?

b. Hopelessly stodgy and dependent?

3. What effects have you noticed since your return from the Second Vatican Council?

a. Wild-eyed rebels charging around in all directions trying to ruin the Church?

b. Apathetic masses scarcely aware that anything has happened?

4. You think nuns ought to go to bed—

a. By 10:30?

b. By themselves?

5. Some of the priests in your diocese are demonstrating against the Vietnam War.

    a. Do you quiet them down before people lose the impression that Catholics are more patriotic than anybody?

    b. Do you tell the non-demonstrators, "9 A.M. Saturday at City Hall or else"?

6. You sent a secret letter to your pastors. Somehow the newspapers obtained a copy and printed it. What did you do then?

    a. Denounce the sensation-mongering press for its distortion of the news?

    b. Congratulate yourself on the success of your sure-fire public relations stratagem?

7. How do you feel when people kneel to kiss your ring?

    a. Do you recall that you are, after all, a successor to the Apostles?

    b. Are you embarrassed because you lost your ring in the park at the "be-in"?

8. When civil rights demonstrations erupt in your diocese, what action do you take?

    a. Do you issue a statement decrying violence and supporting peace and justice?

    b. Do you find the priest most involved in stirring up protest and put him in charge of human relations for the diocese?

9. How do you handle requests for permission to experiment with the liturgy?

    a. Do you turn them down for fear the experimenters will wind up putting pot in the incense burners?

    b. Do you suggest they use some imagination and come up with something better than a new banjo arrangement of the same old hymns?

10. Although your diocesan newspaper operates in the red, do you subsidize it because—

    a. It provides more jobs for priests?

    b. It's still less expensive than reaching the people with television commercials?

SCORING:

If more than half your answers are *a*'s—If you're not careful, you'll have to stand the expense of another trip to Rome for another Council.

If more than half your answers are *b*'s—You'll never make Cardinal.

Personality Test for Popes

(PUBLISHER'S NOTE: This section will be added in a later edition. Our consultants advised us, after a careful study of the material submitted by Mr. Frisbie, that the test appeared to be slanted to favor applicants who were middle-aged authors with brown eyes living in Arlington Heights, Illinois, with a wife, eight children, a dog and a duck. We then queried Mr. Frisbie whether he actually intended to propose such a startling break with tradition. He replied that in a weak moment it seemed desirable to him to be able to order the Swiss Guards to go make everybody shut up for a change, but was feeling stronger now and would revise the papal personality test.)

Full Fathom Five Their Father Fibs

One evening I was sitting in my book-lined study trying to stop a crack where the wind whistled in with a copy of *Wuthering Heights*. I heard a shuffle of feet behind me and turned to find myself confronted by a grievance committee representing the children. They stated three complaints:

1. It had come to their attention that I was continuing to write books and articles in which I used their names. This would tend to expose them to public ridicule and obloquy. They clearly had grounds to sue me for libel, slander, invasion of privacy, mopery and perhaps alienation of affection.

2. If I persisted, they wanted a bigger cut of the proceeds,

"if any," muttered one of them, who had become precociously wise in the ways of the wicked world from reading back issues of *Publishers Weekly* secretly at night in the attic.

3. They had noticed certain instances when my account of an event did not agree with their recollection of the facts. By leaving such exaggerated manuscripts around where they couldn't help prying open the locked drawer and reading them, I was setting a bad example and corrupting their innocent young minds.

For once, I was able to extricate myself from a grievance-committee session without paying double allowances all round. I agreed to stop using their real names. (This is why twenty or thirty children appear in different pieces I have written. I actually have eight children. They only seem like thirty.) In return, they settled for their usual cut of the royalties—one hundred per cent, less the cost of paper and postage.

On the third point, I delivered what I thought was a brilliant rebuttal. I said the essential skill in making a living as a writer is the ability to remember things better than they happened. I conceded that to a scientist, an accident witness or someone responsible for dealing with literal facts, an accurate memory could be useful. But for most of mankind an accurate memory is a burden to its owner and a curse to his family.

"No, it wasn't Henry's car that Mary rode to Aunt Hester's funeral in. She rode with George. I can clearly remember her handing George the crank to start the engine with."

I gave them the example of a friend who went to Ireland. He had relatives there, so he made their homes the base for his sight-seeing expeditions. He soon noticed that the entire family invariably gathered round him as soon as he returned.

"And what did you see today, John?"

"I went for a walk along the Shannon and took a tour of the castle."

"Did you see anyone?"

"There was hardly anyone around. Just the caretaker."

"Did he say anything to you?"

"Only about six words. He just took my money, let me in and went back to reading his newspaper."

"No tourists?"

"Oh, yes. There were a couple of families going through while I was there."

"Did you talk to them?"

"No."

Everyone sat silently. Then one of the cousins asked, "What were they like?"

"I didn't particularly notice. I was enjoying the view from the tower most of the time they were there."

Another long pause. Then the relatives began to excuse themselves and drift away. John sensed that he was disappointing them, but he didn't know why until his closest cousin took him aside one day and explained:

"It's not like America here, John. We don't have the telly and all. There's not much to do but talk. So when you come back from a trip and tell them about it, spin it a little."

Once pointed in the right direction, John's imagination easily filled in myriad details that previously had escaped his observation. During the next week his heightened awareness of his surroundings turned up no fewer than five leprechauns, two of whom spoke to him, and a ghost who followed him all the way back from Blarney Castle singing *Danny Boy* in a remarkably clear tenor voice.

"And what did you see today, John?"

"I walked along the Shannon till I came to the old monastery. I'd read in the guide book that they used to take refuge in the tower when the Vikings came raiding. I thought I'd climb to the top and imagine how the countryside must have looked in those days.

"But I couldn't get in; the door seemed to be locked. While I stood there looking up at the tower, a cloud came over the sun. I felt a cold wind spring up. Then, suddenly, the door blew open."

"Did you go in?"

"Yes. It was dark inside the base of the tower. There was just enough light coming through the little windows at the top for me to see which stairs were missing. I started climbing. About halfway up, I heard something behind me."

"What did it sound like, John?"

"As if someone else were climbing the stairs, too. I could hear the feet shuffling, step . . . step . . . step . . . slowly, the way an old man would climb. And it was a metallic sound. I could hear creakings and clankings, as if pieces of metal were rubbing and knocking together."

"A Viking!" gasped one of the younger cousins.

"Hush now, Bridget, let Cousin John get on with the story."

"I climbed on to the top as fast as I could. Up there, part of the roof was missing so there was plenty of light. I stood and waited to see who or what was following me. I heard the steps coming closer and closer, closer and closer—"

At this point, there were so many of my own children clutching me that I couldn't breathe enough to finish the story of John's visit to Ireland, but I felt they understood my point. I said that if the art of conversation languishes in our times, it is because people who may be fanciful enough in their discussions of foreign affairs, politics and race relations are determined to hang, draw and quarter every hair of their daily lives with merciless accuracy. And this is ridiculous because every thoughtful person knows that important truths are too big to be contained in literal facts and must instead be conveyed by way of myth.

The children didn't seem to follow the thought about myths being truer than facts. "You mean it's all right to fib?" one of them said.

I denied having granted such license and tried to explain. No one, I said, tells a more plausible story than a confidence man about to separate you from your life savings. The conventional and expected story goes unquestioned just when it should be investigated by the grand jury. As artists and philosophers have always known, the most interesting truths are found in the most unlikely places.

They still didn't understand.

So I put to them the case of a person who knows perfectly well there is no such thing as a leprechaun, but thinks it's splendid when you tell him you saw one smoking its little pipe at sundown in the park.

"Where?" they exclaimed.

"By the fountain."

Then they all ran out to play with the leprechaun and left me in peace. By a remarkable coincidence, it turned out to be a cousin of the leprechauns that spoke to John in Ireland. The whole lot of them came from County Clare.

The Summer of My Discontent

June 18

This morning I decided once again that I should try to keep a journal. Writers are expected to keep journals. If you have one, you can jot down ideas as they occur to you and write about them later when you have time.

I read in today's newspaper, for example, that University of Chicago researchers have defined a happy family as one with "the ability to dispel tensions." I must write about this. I mentioned the article to my wife, and we agreed we have often remarked the necessity for techinques to dispel tensions.

At our house, I'm the one who tends to wake up cheerful, which is not invariably the mood of other members of the family. One day when the group at breakfast was growlier than usual, I decided to pretend we were being visited by the Cheer-up Bird, a magical being whose mere presence scatters sunshine and smiles in all directions.

My performance as the Cheer-up Bird almost defies description. It is a blend of ballet, opera, pantomime and the circus.

Four robins, two grackles and a red-eyed vireo perched on
the window sill to watch. The neighbor child who always rings
the backdoor bell at 7:30 A.M. ran home to get her little sister
so she could see it, too. The milkman and two garbage collectors
burst into spontaneous applause. The coffee, although accidentally left on a cold burner, heated itself up thirty degrees.

The older children turned pale and speechless. Even young
Attila hid his face in his mother's apron.

Obviously, I had hit upon an effective tension-dispelling
technique. It's so effective that I never have had to repeat the
performance. When there seems to be tension at the breakfast
table, I just offer to be the Cheer-up Bird again.

"OK, OK, we're cheerful," the children say at once. "Look,
we're laughing."

June 29

Today I discovered there are at least two secret passageways
in our house, perhaps three.

This is the only possible explanation for some of the things
that go on here. I have known for a long time that one of the
secret passageways originates somewhere upstairs and leads
through an underground tunnel to an exit concealed in the
backyard. I have tried unsuccessfully to find it many times. But
it must be there. How else could Enrico be singing noisily upstairs one minute, then, seconds later, when I want to send him
on an errand, have vanished without coming down the stairs?

I have now deduced that a second secret passageway must
emerge behind the cedar paneling in the remodeled porch we call
a study. Since I nailed up the paneling myself when we remodeled, it is all the more mysterious that there could be a
secret passageway I didn't discover when the room was stripped
to its studs.

Nevertheless, there must be one. No matter how carefully
I watch, various unknown persons are able to slip into the
room and escape without being seen. If I put down a roll of
cellophane tape on my desk, it disappears the first time I blink.

The same is true of ballpoint pens. And the users of the secret passageway apparently can smell scissors; they got away even with the pair I hid under the radiator.

I'm not sure yet about the third passageway. If it exists, it would explain how I can be the only person in the house until I start for the bathroom—whereupon I always find it occupied. I suspect there may be a secret door behind the tile. The wall sounds hollow when I tap a certain place over the tub.

July 10

Few families can guarantee that every member will receive all communications promptly. Although mail isn't much of a problem, "call-me-back" telephone messages can be tricky.

Writing messages on the refrigerator door works only if you can find a pencil (all pencils having been lost the first week after school let out). I have already explained why there are no ballpoints in the house. That leaves chalk—attached to a small blackboard with a piece of string.

The problem with blackboard and chalk is getting the messages erased afterward so that everyone doesn't have to return the same calls over and over.

Once we tried a family "mail box" with separate sections for each member. But after a time the compartments became so full of roller-skate keys, butterfly collections and wet bathing suits that there wasn't room for messages.

Consequently, the children have learned to use their ingenuity when an important message has to be transmitted. Last night when the parents came home late, there was a note painted on the refrigerator door in purple Lifetyme Enamel: "Call Mr. Garcia, 429-3860."

The same message was written on the bathroom mirror in lipstick, spelled out in blocks on the kitchen floor, scrawled across the dining room table in peanut butter and embroidered on our pillows. (Another copy, taped to the six pack in the refrigerator as a last resort, wasn't found till several minutes later.)

So I called Mr. Garcia at 2 A.M. He was selling awnings. I didn't buy any, and he didn't seem much interested in continuing the conversation.

July 23

A neighbor stopped at our house last night while searching for his children, who were half an hour late for dinner. "I'm always late for everything myself," he said, "but I'm going to teach my children to be punctual or bust."

I dived immediately for the fallout shelter.

There it occurred to me that the heaviest burden of parenthood is the obligation of always being an Example. You can't talk children into much; you have to lead them. Consequently, parents' lives are as public as if the whole house were bugged like an American embassy.

I was reminded of the time I was discarding a handful of old credit cards, financial records and other documents best kept out of the hands of strangers. I put them into the leaf burner and struck a match. My son Jeremiah popped out of the nearby shrubbery with a question:

"Didn't you tell me it was against the law in our town to burn anything but leaves?"

Another day, while driving down a long, steep grade, I inadvertently allowed the car to gather speed for a few hundred yards. Jerry, who had been sound asleep in the back seat till that moment, suddenly arose like one of the Just at the Last Judgment and trumpeted:

"You're going forty-eight miles an hour and the sign says the speed limit is forty-five!"

Last night at dinner, after the neighbor had left without either busting or finding his children, we began discussing the importance of conserving our natural resources. I should have known what to expect.

This morning when I was brushing my teeth, a small hand whipped around in front of me and turned off the cold water faucet. "You're wasting water," a righteous voice proclaimed.

Rattled, I crept off to breakfast with my mouth still tasting of toothpaste.

August 15

Parents who do not own a dog should realize before they buy one that the dog will always side with the children, and vice versa. They must not be misled by stories like *Peter Pan*, in which the dog was on the parents' side and tried to snitch on the children. This never happens in real life.

Today, I found one of our typewriters knocked over. Whether the dog was to blame or a child is beside the point. I picked up the machine and typed out the traditional phrase for testing the keys of the alphabet:

"The quick brown fox jumps over the lazy dog."

Satisfied that all was well, I went out, leaving the paper in the typewriter.

The local branch of the League Against Slurs on Curs was offended. When I returned, I found that an anonymous author had appended one more line on the same sheet of paper:

"It was the dum (sic) fox got jumped over."

September 20

I must be more faithful about making entries in my journal. It is a well-known fact that every writer keeps a journal. A journal is useful for jotting down things that happen to you which you'd be better off forgetting if you weren't a writer.

No Magic on Weekends

Many parents are unaware of the menace lurking in libraries and bookstores. These iniquitous institutions harbor innumerable children's books full of the lore of necromancy, complete with how-to-do-it instructions. Children who read by the hour about turning enemies into lizards, transmitting hay to gold or flying on magic carpets naturally want to try such enchanting sports.

I have warned many friends and neighbors about the dangers of allowing such books in the house, but they all deny that magic exists. They close their eyes to the plain evidence that children are working spells all around them day and night.

My own daughter, Titania, already has a considerable repertory, which is the reason I have been forced to make a strict rule at our house prohibiting magic on weekends. If she and the other children wish to practice spells when I'm not around, that's permitted. One must not discourage children's creativity. But on weekends when I am home, I insist on a certain respect for reality.

Taney's first big success was the enchanted stick trick, popularized several years ago by the play, *Mrs. McThing*. My wife and I were foolish enough to discuss the play in front of Taney, and somehow she figured out how to work the trick.

One casts a spell on a piece of willow wood about three feet long. The spell turns the stick into an exact replica of the sorcerer, leaving him free to travel while the stick-replica occupies his usual place, doing his usual chores in a mechanical way. (I won't tell you the words of the incantation; it wouldn't be in the public interest.)

I first realized Taney could do the stick trick one day when I spoke to her in the yard. She ostensibly was lying on her back under a pear tree, staring up at the ripening pears glistening in the afternoon sun. I asked her to run to the garage and fetch my pruning shears. She didn't stir. I looked at her more closely and concluded from the glassy stare in her eyes that I was talking to a stick-replica. The real Taney was a thousand miles away. Since shears-fetching was not routine, the replica couldn't do it.

Numerous incidents of this sort over a period of time led me to speculate about Taney's mode of transportation. I kept the broom under strict surveillance to no avail. She didn't use it even to sweep with (unless I insisted strongly that it was her turn to clean the kitchen). Only gradually did it occur to me that travel in the fifth dimension, for adepts, is simply a matter of tuning out the workaday world. I should have known Taney would scorn a cliché like a broomstick.

Children do not acquire their magical skills overnight. Considerable practice is required before the spells come out right every time. In the beginning the spells often misfire, which is a frustration to the children and a nuisance to the parents. Half the appliances in our house have been inadvertently hexed at one time or another.

The dishwasher harbors a magically inexhaustible spring. The wet kind. Underneath the machinery is a rubber receptacle about the size of a saucepan into which the water drains on its way to the discharge pump. From time to time, I have to loosen the connections and fish inside the rubber receptacle to remove an olive pit or a pork chop bone or someone's eyeglasses, lodged there after a thorough washing.

The first step is to siphon any remaining dishwater from the rubber receptacle. It appears to hold about a quart. Actually, it is bottomless. I have many times siphoned out thirty or forty gallons, only to be swept away by a gushing torrent as soon as I loosened the pump connection.

I think that one of the children's stray hexes has annoyed the water nymph in charge of the spring and made her vengeful. That's why the dishwater flood contains globules of gravy when all we had for dinner was waffles.

The clothes washer also is hexed. When the machine can be persuaded to run, the clothes suffer a sea-change of color and pattern. A garment that goes in as a simple white shirt may come out as the multi-hued coronation gown of the Princess of Barataria.

Then there are the turn signals on the car. Although the right turn blinkers always work, the other side has fallen afoul of foul play. The lights refuse to signal a left turn in damp weather. I have tried and tried to have them fixed without success. The last mechanic said a little man with a green beard popped out at him from under the dashboard and threatened to turn him into a black stone. I have learned from experience with Taney's weird associates that a green beard is a sign of a touchy disposition. So, in rainy weather, I just roll down the window and stick my arm out into the downpour to signal a left turn. That's better than being turned into a black stone.

I have grown somewhat resigned to these inconveniences, partly because they occur less frequently now that Titania and the other children are more skillful at keeping their spells on target. I might not have banned the practice of the black arts on weekends if Taney had not tried to turn her little brother into a toad.

I'll admit he can be rather a bother, and Taney no doubt was grossly provoked. But that's no excuse for anti-social behavior. What if she couldn't find the right spell to turn him back into a boy? Even the most sensible children have moments of irresponsibility.

I could hear Taney shouting upstairs. She was saying something like, "Hop down off my dresser before I croak you." I rushed up the stairs, fortunately arriving before she had time to recite the incantation. (The Toad incantation is rather long.) Having restored order, I laid down my new rules:

1. No one is to be turned into a toad, not even little brothers.

2. When new children's books come into the house, the spells they contain are to be practiced outdoors, to avoid accidental hexing of appliances.

3. No magic whatever is to be worked when I am home, which automatically eliminates weekends.

Then, tired from the tension of the scene, I went back downstairs and took my afternoon nap on the living-room sofa. I think Taney was annoyed at my firmness. Maybe that's why I slept a hundred years.

Rue, Rue, Rue Your Boat

Taking a child out in a boat nowadays makes even the shortest
trip a slow voyage in the horse latitudes. Social and technological
changes are spoiling the fun. With boats in every garage, little
old ladies own seventy-five-horsepower motors and have learned
to water ski on one foot.

It was different when I was a boy growing up on the shores
of Lake Michigan. Then, any sort of sea-going conveyance that
held a boy up in the water without swimming was considered
a yacht. Whenever a water-logged length of piling drifted up
on the beach, we would nail old license plates or flattened
cans to sticks to make paddles and set out on long voyages,
undismayed by the tendency of old piling either to roll us off
into the surf or to sink under our weight until we found ourselves trying to paddle with the water around our shoulders.

Any boy who owned an inflatable inner tube felt entitled to
swagger along the waterfront like a Bermuda Race winner.

We learned to swim. Not with the style, perhaps, that children nowadays are taught in the park pool or the YMCA but
with a good deal more versatility. We had to cope with the
lake in all of its moods.

One mood is Cold. Lake Michigan always maintains an
Arctic chill until the end of July. By the end of August it is
already cooling off again for winter. In between there may be
a few days when the water reaches seventy degrees—as long as
the wind doesn't blow offshore. An offshore breeze pushes the
sun-warmed surface water out into the middle of the lake and
pulls in from the depths water of such single-minded, unre-
lenting coldness that four penguins who had escaped from the

Lincoln Park Zoo into Lake Michigan once froze to death
on the first of August.

We did not mind the extreme difficulty of paddling a piece
of water-logged piling with a flattened can on a stick; only by
such frantic activity could we keep ourselves warm.

Another mood is Wavy. A steady breeze off the lake makes
the air cold but brings in water of whatever warmth is to be
had that week. Occasionally, such a wind may blow for several
days. This has the effect of piling up surf of increasing vigor
until it is finally too rough for anyone to swim in.

Since we were used to battling whitecaps, we would continue
going to the beach every day regardless. I remember how I
could tell when the waves finally were too big. As soon as I
waded in, a huge wave would rise above my head and crash
down on me with a roar like thunder. The undertow around
my ankles would yank my feet from under me. Then the
turbulent currents would roll me over and over two or three
times, scraping my knees, elbows and shoulders roughly against
the bottom. By the time the wave had spent its force, I would
be fifty yards down the beach from where I started, with sand
in my ears, seaweed draped around my neck and a dead perch
in my mouth.

The lake's other principal mood was Polluted. A variety of
strange substances sometimes would drift down on us from the
steel mills and other heavy industries concentrated at the south
end of Lake Michigan. There wasn't much we could do about
oil, but we became quite adept at swimming through acres of
floating slag. The trick was to splash it out of the way with one
hand while swimming with the other. A similar technique was
effective when some chemical killed a few million minnows.
However, after an afternoon of swimming through floating
minnows, we were likely to be followed home by cats.

An invitation to ride in a real boat would have kept any boy
of my generation wide awake with excitement the night before.
The modern children of my acquaintance can be induced to go
boating only when they have nothing else in particular to do

and the weather is especially fine. I grew up in such simple times that children even looked forward to the Saturday afternoon movies—the same movies that now, on television, don't hold children's attention long enough for the parents to finish a cocktail undisturbed.

The children aren't to blame. A few generations ago a kid could be kept in line by his parents for months by a hint that he might get a single well-traveled orange in his stocking at Christmas if he behaved himself and did all his chores with a willing spirit. Today's children spit orange juice at each other every morning of their lives, and to persuade them to deliver a high output of child-power, you have to promise them a sockful of more than oranges. This is what the sociologists mean when they talk about "post-affluent youth."

Even though intellectually I can see they are a product of their times, emotionally I have no sympathy with anyone who can be blasé about boating.

For a long time, I put off buying a family boat. I was discouraged every time I calculated the size of the vessel required to accommodate all the children, their friends and their animals. Where do you go to buy a sand-and-gravel barge? But it turned out that a seventeen-foot sailing canoe was quite large enough for everyone willing to risk an encounter with water that might be wavy or cold—or wet.

One pleasant Saturday in July, I provisioned the boat and cast off with a crew consisting of my son Chris and a tall friend of his named John. The wind was just strong enough to send us skimming along at a delightful speed without threatening to tip the lee rail under at the first relaxation of vigilance. Since the wind lay abeam, we didn't even have to worry about fighting contrary winds when the time came to start home. A cabin cruiser did pass rather close to us with an enormous wake, but we managed to take it bow on. Afterward, we sank the miscreant with one broadside.

When we were well out on the lake, I ordered lunch served to all hands. Christian and Long John immediately complained because there was no jelly in the peanut butter sandwiches. Sternly (that's where I was sitting, in the stern), I reminded them of the heroic traditions of the sea. Would Columbus, who said, "Sail on, sail on," have complained because there was no jelly in a peanut butter sandwich? Wouldn't Admiral Farragut, who said, "Damn the torpedoes," have said, in the present circumstances, "Damn the jelly!"? Since Admiral Farragut wasn't there, I said it for him. The crew's only reaction was to reproach me further for having forgotten the salt for the hard-boiled eggs.

After a time, our course took us past an island, which was thickly wooded. The trees cut off much of the wind, slowing our speed. As the canoe inched along with the sail only partly drawing, the crew complained of the heat and demanded to know why we hadn't steered to windward of the island.

I didn't want to admit I simply hadn't thought of it because of the fuss about the food, so I changed the subject. Gazing at the bright waters ahead, I recalled that this particular small lake was joined—like the Great Lakes—to the Mississippi by a system of inland waterways. I told them that with a couple of short portages around dams at the outset we could sail to New Orleans, then across the Gulf, through the Panama Canal and into the Pacific. From Panama, I said, it would be only 70,000 or 80,000 miles to Tahiti.

More grumbling from the crew. "We didn't sign on for Tahiti," they objected. "Besides, we want to get home in time to watch at least part of the ballgame on television."

"Mr. Christian, this is mutiny!" I bellowed. Chris and Long John quailed before my stern gaze. (I was still sitting in the stern.) Shortly, however, I heard them whispering behind the apple barrel that stood amidship. I knew I would have to act quickly or they would slip me the Black Spot.

Once before I had set out for Tahiti, but my inner tube had sprung a leak and sunk in a raging storm off the Seventy-second Street breakwater in four feet of water. This time it was the crew that stood in the way. So I pinned a note to Chris' collar saying I would be late for dinner. Then I threw both of the lily-livered swabs overboard and sailed on to Tahiti alone.

Richard Frisbie and His Giant Magnet

One sure way to get your children into good colleges, with perhaps a fat foundation grant besides, is to cultivate their interest in science. A young man who seems to have a knack for astrophysics can choose for himself the best room on the campus. Some of the better schools would dislodge even a promising halfback to accommodate a first-class piece of scientific talent.

At our house, we keep trying to increase the nation's pool of scientific childpower. Considering our investment in laboratory supplies, I rather expected someone in the family would have discovered a new element before now. Or at least brought home an A in Science just once.

But somehow our experiments always come out peculiar, more like Jonathan Swift's satires than Tom Swift's successes. My wife, who claims it is all my fault, frequently mentions the episode of the venus flytraps. After I had spent weeks and weeks growing them in a flowerpot, we invited them to dinner in celebration of their reaching maturity. I still don't see how I can be blamed because the greedy creatures ate too much roast beef and died of indigestion.

One spring I brought home a bucket of pond water. It was full of tiny animals just visible without magnification. Day by day, as we watched, the bigger specks ate the smaller specks and grew still bigger. I had intended to buy whatever kind of field guide is needed to identify pond water specks, but

before I could get around to it, the children poured all the
specks down the drain. They said the biggest speck had snapped
viciously at our dog.

I have an eerie feeling I wouldn't have found any pictures
of *those* pond water denizens in the field guide anyway.

We have just as much trouble with the supposedly exact
physical sciences as we do with the branches of biology. The
more we dabble with the laws of the universe the closer we
come to demonstrating that Einstein, Newton, Galileo, Archi-
medes and the rest had it all backwards.

For instance, I had always been taught that metal *expands*
when heated. One night I tried to demonstrate this for the
children. Following the instructions in a Junior Science book,
we measured a long piece of copper wire, heated it with candles
at several points and measured it again. At first we could detect
no change in length. I went to the basement for more candles
and created a fire storm under that wire. A couple of candles
more would have melted it. When we measured it again, it
was two inches *shorter* than before I lit the first candle.

Subsequently, it was suggested to me that certain members
of my audience harbored a disrespectful attitude toward science.
One of them, with the connivance of the others, could have
snipped off a piece of the wire while I was in the basement
getting candles. I don't believe it. My own theory (assuming
that conventional physics is correct) is that the hardware store
sold me stale wire.

I'm not going to trade at that hardware store any more.
I don't have to. I have discovered the Edmund Scientific Co.,
which publishes a fat catalogue and will mail me anything from
surplus dental tools to a two-thousand-degree solar furnace. (I
bet that furnace would lengthen a copper wire.)

One item we bought from the catalogue was a hemispherical
device with a light inside that projects a star map on the
ceiling of a darkened room. We used to lie on the floor of
our do-it-yourself planetarium picking out Cassiopeia, Corona,
Draco and the new constellation we discovered, which turned

out to be the result of dropping the projector. An ill fate eventually caught up with this star-crossed machine, and it became an instrument of vengeance. When we switched it on one night, a whole new galaxy—added that afternoon with an ice pick—spelled out across the heavens: PETEY IS AN ASTRONUT.

Our next purchase was an inexpensive opaque projector. It magnifies and projects on our movie screen an image not only of drawings and photographs but also of anything else small enough to fit under its mirror. This makes it useful for studying leaves, fossils, seashells, mineral specimens and other instructive objects with a group. (We do seem to concentrate on the theatrics of science.)

I was delighted to discover that the children used this projector frequently. Until a time when I heard them giggling in a way that would make any experienced parent suspicious. I burst in and caught them projecting the roller-skating scabs on their knees (enlarged to two or three feet across) and taking votes for the ugliest. "That won't get you into Harvard," I shouted. To emphasize my disapproval of such frivolity, I made them spend the rest of the evening counting caterpillar legs.

Despite experiences like this, I remain convinced that scientific birthday gifts can do much to stimulate a young person's mind. Just the other day, I was thumbing through the catalogue with our kindergartener, Icarius. I had to admit I couldn't afford the infrared sniperscope that lets one see in the dark, but I directed Ickie's attention to several other exciting possibilities. A ninety-degree prism that makes a camera turn corners and take photos while people think you're pointing it away from them. Photocells that can be rigged up to turn the lights on and off or open doors.

"And look," I said. "Here's a magnet that weighs less than sixteen pounds and can lift 350 pounds. Isn't that fascinating?"

Ickie said, "Will it get me into Harvard?"

I still think somebody put him up to it. I know a frame-up when I see one.

The Light Behind the Furnace

The last time we moved I thought we might have to wind up in a tribal long house in Borneo. It takes a heap of house hunting to find a home with the thirty-foot kitchen needed for a large family like ours. After a time, most of the houses begin to look alike and we found ourselves wondering if each shack wasn't the same place we looked at last month.

However, some houses reveal intimate glimpses of eccentric people that are as interesting as a Dickens novel.

We were in one house that had a shooting gallery under the living room. The area was only partly excavated. A marksman could stand in the basement, slide open a panel opening onto the crawl space and fire at the target. It was ingeniously mounted on a trolley so it could be retrieved for inspection like wash on a clothesline. After the bullet passed through the target, it was deflected into the earth by a large plate of steel, possibly filched from a battleship.

This was the house that started us guessing about the former inhabitants of the dwellings we visited.

"Who do you suppose lived here?" my wife said.

"Some kind of a nut," I answered.

"Hush, the realtor will hear you."

"A John Bircher," I continued. "Or a Minute Man. I bet he used to cut pictures of people he didn't like out of the newspapers and shoot them for practice."

My wife disagreed. She visualized the proprietor of the shooting gallery as a country gentleman, forced by untoward circumstances to live in the suburbs. Shooting at the target was his way of keeping his eye sharp against the day he could be back among the grouse on his beloved moors.

We compromised on an explorer. Preparing to collect man-eating snails at the headwaters of the Amazon, he had been improving his aim so if necessary he could hit a piranha-fish in the left eye at forty paces.

The next place had a peculiarity we didn't notice at first. It seemed like an ordinary house, comfortable enough except for the tiny, cramped kitchen. Gradually we realized there was no refrigerator in the house, and no place to put one. After half an hour of measuring and considering various possible arrange-ments, we concluded that if we wanted a standard-sized re-frigerator in that house, we'd have to keep it in the basement or the dining room. The kitchen seemed designed purposely to exclude any possibility of a refrigerator.

My wife guessed that the former owners were in the restaurant business and never ate at home. I guessed that the man of the house had been stationed in England during the war and con-ceived an obsessive prejudice against cold beer as a result of having been deprived of it for inhumanly long periods. We compromised on a retired farmer who had built the house when he was 120 years old and never happened to have heard that refrigerators had been invented.

Then there was the house with the twigs for curtain rods. It had been solidly constructed in an era of sound craftsman-ship, but small details of the hardware were incredibly make-shift. The householders had been inclined to bend a nail into some weird shape and make do rather than spend twenty-nine cents at the hardware store.

"They were hard up during the Depression," I theorized. "This is an example of the pioneer spirit that built America. If you can't afford store-boughten hardware, you just whittle an inventive device out of hardrock maple. Abe Lincoln would have understood."

My wife snorted. "I know cheapskates when I see them.

And hanging curtains on splintery old dirty twigs is not what I call inventive."

Another house had an electrical mystery in the basement. There was a wall switch just inside the door in the expected place, but it didn't control the nearby ceiling light, which was rigged with a pull-chain. Instead, the wall switch controlled only a single light at the far end of the basement behind the furnace.

Evolving a theory to fit this case took much thought. Finally, we agreed it was the work of a woman, possibly with a husband who traveled on business week in and week out. She developed a fixation that someday someone—or SOMETHING—would pop out from behind the furnace and get her while she was washing the clothes. So she called an electrician and had the light behind the furnace wired to the wall switch; then the Thing could be frightened away by the light the instant she entered the basement.

"But the Thing got her after all," I said, "and that's why the house is for sale."

"Let's go," my wife said. "You've done it again. I couldn't possibly live in this house worrying all the time what might be behind that furnace."

At one point, after looking at a particularly unpromising series of aged houses, we contacted an architect about the possibility of building a new house to our own specifications. He spent an evening with us, taking notes on the various special features that would make the house an expression of our family's unique personality.

Besides the usual features, there would be a dark room, a sewing room, music-practice rooms, a home theater with spotlights for amateur productions and a projection booth, utility space to house reptiles, amphibians and small mammals, bookshelves in every room including, or especially, kitchen and bath—

"Speaking of baths," I interrupted, "would it be possible to arrange for two very large showers, one for the boys and one for the girls? In this family everyone always wants to take a bath at the same time."

An expression came over the architect's face which I have seen many times on men in fields like his. It means: "It's your money, buster."

I continued. "Also, how about steel crash doors like the ones on a ship? When the children get to fighting we can isolate the affected area by shutting the doors and dogging them down."

He went away to draft a rough plan.

A few weeks later he telephoned. "I've worked in everything you wanted, Mr. Frisbie, but you won't like it."

I asked him how he could be so sure I wouldn't like it when I hadn't even seen the plan. He'd already said he'd managed to put in all the features we wanted.

"Well, you have to agree there are many unusual details in this house."

He had us there.

"In order to fit them together at a price that would make any sense at all, I could design the house only one way. You may not believe this, Mr. Frisbie, but it looks just like a shoe!"

Our first reaction was suspicion. Then, reading the writings of Frank Lloyd Wright, we stopped doubting the competence of our architect. The great Wright apparently had stubbed his toe on a similar project once in his career. No family should have more than two children, Wright had written, if they want an architect to design a proper house for them. The trouble was not with our architect but with our family.

We finally bought an old house with unusual details of its own, like pipes that aren't attached to anything (Abstract Plumbing) and a study floor that slopes like the deck of a ship under sail (It's a TRIP, man). Someday we may build our dream house after all. Meanwhile, we have shelter and plenty of time to decide whether we would prefer a brogan or an oxford.

Why They Never Leave the Honey
on the Porch in Duluth

One Sunday afternoon we were picnicking in a woods near
our house in a suburb of Chicago. The late fall weather, sunny
but cold, had kept the transistor-radio crowd at home. Unused
to being in the woods with no one else around, the younger
children began to notice the sounds. A sudden scampering in
the crisp fallen leaves. The unexplained crack of a dry twig.
Something falling to the ground with a thud. Timorously, they
asked whether there could be any bears in the vicinity.

Fortunately, I was able to assure them that all the wild
bears in the United States east of the Rocky Mountains live in
or near Duluth, Minnesota.

Quite a few cities, usually thought of as highly urbanized,
are known for attracting various forms of wildlife. The South
Side of Chicago often looks like West Texas because of its
roaming herds of wild steers. The steers are always escaping from
pens in the stockyards or from cattle trucks that have accidents.
Policemen regularly assigned to the area have become expert
cowboys. They get more practice rounding up loose steers than
many genuine ranch hands.

It's a spectacle to see a frisky dogie loping down alleys,
leaping fences, dashing through thickets of clotheslines and
knocking over garbage cans, with two or three squads of police
following every twist and turn of the trail.

"Car 312, Car 312 . . . head him off at the pass. That is
all."

Years ago, before the Chicago stockyards began to cut back
their operations, there was a police sergeant, Tex Murphy, so

good at bulldogging that he gave exhibitions at rodeos. No one would compete against him because no one else could do it his way. Murphy's method was to drive alongside a running steer, reach out the window with a nightstick in his left hand and knock the animal cold with one smack behind the right ear. He missed only once. That was the time in Madison Square Garden when a big Brahman ducked at the moment of truth and butted Tex and his trained squad car, Old Paint, into the fifth row.

Tucson, Arizona, I will always remember for its lizards. They are pretty little creatures about three inches long. They can be quiescent, perching on your head without moving for a long time, but when you realize they're there and grab for them they scoot away faster than a blink. Every block in Tucson has thousands of them darting through the oleanders and cacti or crawling on the window screens.

The lizards are friendly and harmless enough, but having them everywhere is a bit disconcerting. I used to resent it when one of them would fall into a fresh highball and thrash around until half the whiskey was wasted. When you drank the rest of it, the taste was never the same. Once I put my hand into my pocket to pay for something at the store and found myself giving the sales clerk a dollar bill, two dimes, a nickel, three pennies and six lizards.

Several towns in Florida, I understand, are noted for an abundance of alligators, especially in the kind of area where people build homes with individual piers on private lakes. The alligators are quite loyal. All you have to do is push a fat dog or cat off the pier from time to time, and the alligators will become tame and hang around indefinitely.

I learned the surprising facts about Duluth and its black bears many years ago while working as a newspaper editor. Needing a photograph of a bear to illustrate a feature article, I sent a copyboy to the paper's photo library. He returned with two bulging envelopes marked "Bears."

Nearly all the pictures proved to be wire service photos originating in Duluth. Reading the captions, I learned that when black bears wake from their hibernation in early spring, lean and hungry, they leave their dens in the woods and stroll into Duluth to see what's for breakfast. Apparently, the bears and the people in Duluth tolerate each other rather well.

I recall only one shot of a fracas. Police had to remove one bear from Miss Ethyl Olsen's back porch, where he had eaten an upside-down cake and two mouthfuls of the broom she poked him with. While being hustled off to the bear pound, the bear stuck out his tongue at the photographer.

There is a long precedent for some kinds of bears and people getting along together. European bears allow gypsies to teach them to dance in the market place and display less ferocity than the average organ-grinder's monkey. Our American black bears at Yellowstone and other western national parks are patient with the tourists, biting only a couple a day during the season to maintain *some* respect for wildlife. On the human side, all kinds of bears are extremely popular at zoos, and millions of children have comforted themselves at bedtime with toy bears. One cannot imagine a market for cuddy toy hyenas. Or aardvarks. Or three-toed sloths.

The photographers in Duluth, well aware of the widespread human affinity for bears, can't pass up shooting more bear pictures every spring. As for the bears, they seem to enjoy posing.

When I spread out the file photos on my desk, I saw bears using every facility a city the size of Duluth (pop. 104,000) could possibly offer, with photographic emphasis on the situations that suggested the humorous captions photo editors love. There was a bear in the ball park, presumably waiting for the Cubs to come to town; a bear in the main department store, looking for moth balls for his fur coat; a bear in the public library, hoping to check out A *Moveable Feast*.

There was one remarkable shot of a big bear and a little bear. The caption said they were walking toward the local observatory. After I thought about this, I decided that either Duluth doesn't have an observatory or the bears never actually went there. No photographer would have missed a chance to snap Ursus Major and Ursus Minor together on the steps of the observatory.

After I explained all this, the children wanted to know whether I had ever been to Duluth to see the bears myself. I said I expected to visit that city eventually. Air travel, to which I am sometimes forced to subject myself, is full of little surprises like coming down in a city you never expected to see. Sooner or later, I'll be aboard a jet pointed for Chicago in bad weather, we'll overshoot O'Hare Field a mite, and we'll all be in Duluth before we know it.

"What will you do then, Dad?" asked my son Mowgli.

I said I would take advantage of the opportunity to find out how the bears are getting on nowadays in Duluth. I wouldn't be at all surprised to find out that by now they have been trained to take their own pictures.

Using Kodiaks, of course.

The Absolutely Bully Camping Trip

(The following motion picture was awarded the Grand Prix at the Arlington Heights, Illinois, Interplanetary Film Festival, which is not surprising since it was the only entry.)

CAMERA	SOUND
1. FADE IN. We see a rugged outdoor type—John Wayne or Richard Frisbie—preparing for a camping trip. At a kitchen table littered with canned goods and camping gear he is packing food into a knapsack. Provisions include quantities of bubblegum, candy bars and potato chips.	MUSIC: THE SONG OF THE VOYAGEURS, "ALOUETTE," PLAYED BY AN ENSEMBLE OF GUITARS.

2. A bedroom. Three boys, in various stages of getting dressed, are playing catch with a shoe.

3. Back in kitchen we see the shoe come flying through the doorway and land among the provisions. The father picks it up, strides to doorway, seizes (from off screen) the smallest boy, drags him to a chair and puts on his shoe.
DISSOLVE.

4. Portrait of Theodore Roosevelt with title supered: "Everything's Bully."

DISSOLVE.

5. The three boys—Bushwacker, Fafnir and Caliban—run to window and look out.

6. REVERSE ANGLE. Through rain-spattered window we see the three boys looking out. In poses similar to that of T.R. in portrait they all have a "puss on," as some families describe that expression which bodes ill for any enterprise in progress.
DISSOLVE.

7. A campsite in early morning. The rain is over. A large tent is pitched near the type of bench and table generally provided in state and national parks. The tent flap opens, the father

FADE MUSIC UNDER.
NARRATOR: That great outdoorsman, Theodore Roosevelt, recommended two ways to judge when a boy is old enough to go camping. The first test is whether he is old enough to dress himself.

The second test is whether he understands—as Teddy himself used to put it—"when once off, all ills from mosquitoes to a downpour of rain must be borne not only uncomplainingly but cheerfully."

SOUND: THUNDER CRACK, FOLLOWED IMMEDIATELY BY DELUGE OF RAIN. MUSIC SEGUES TO OMINOUS MINOR KEY VARIATION.

MUSIC: PICKS UP CHEERFUL "ALOUETTE" THEME AGAIN. NARRATOR: Whether these boys will live to be old enough is a question, but here they are with their father emerges. He stretches and looks up at the sky.

in the woods, enjoying a healthful, character-building pastime.

8. We begin a series of fast cuts showing the father in various activities. He picks up a bucket.

One basic rule of camping is that every member of the party must do his share.

9. He fills bucket at pump.

10. He lights camp stove.

11. He cracks eggs into frying pan.

12. He butters bread.

13. He pumps camp stove.

14. He sets plates on table.

15. Boys now emerge at a leisurely pace from tent, sit at table and begin eating. DISSOLVE.

Of course, some shares are bigger than others.

16. On the trail. The smallest boy strolls into view carrying only a can opener.

MUSIC: CHANGES TO GROFE'S "ON THE TRAIL" FROM "GRAND CANYON SUITE"

17. The other two boys pass the same spot, each carrying one end of a long stick. From the center of the stick is slung a single one-quart canteen.

An experienced leader delegates as much responsibility as he can.

18. Now the father passes. He is carrying the tent, four sleeping bags, the food bag, the camp stove, an ax and a case of bubblegum. DISSOLVE.

MUSIC: WE COME TO THE PART WHERE THE ORCHESTRA IMITATES THE SOUND OF A BURRO BRAYING.

19. Lunchtime deep in the woods. The father and the three boys are sitting on a log. The father opens a knapsack and distributes sandwiches.

MUSIC: SEGUE TO TYPICAL LIGHT "DINNER" MUSIC.
NARRATOR: Lunchtime on a hike is a wonderful time for a father and his boys to exchange man-

20. Caliban bites his sandwich and makes a face.

21. Bushwacker bites his sandwich and makes a face.

22. Fafnir bites his sandwich and makes a face.

23. Resignedly, the father trades his unbitten sandwich to the nearest boy. Everyone then starts trading sandwiches till we lose track of who has what.

24. We see the three boys eating their sandwiches, PAN to father who is just looking at his.

25. CLOSE UP of father's sandwich. It has three bites out of it. DISSOLVE.

26. Sundown in camp. The father looks at the sky, decides the night is clear and begins unrolling the sleeping bags on the ground, which appears smooth and grassy.

27. Caliban settles comfortably into his sleeping bag.

28. Bushwacker settles comfortably into his sleeping bag.

29. Fafnir settles comfortably into his sleeping bag.

30. Father squirms uncomfortably. Finally climbs out of sleeping bag.

31. We watch over father's shoulder as he peeks under sleeping bag. The grassy turf

to-man conversation while enjoying their food with the zest only vigorous outdoor exercise can give.

MUSIC: SEGUE TO "SWEET AND LOW."
NARRATOR: In good weather, there's nothing more delightful than sleeping out under the stars, resting gently on the soft bosom of Mother Earth at day's end while the breezes and sounds of night lull the tired campers to sleep.

underneath has unaccountably
turned into pebbles and gravel.
He looks up in sudden alarm.

SOUND: THE BUZZ OF A
SINGLE MOSQUITO, WHICH
BECOMES A CHORUS AND
SEGUES TO THE SOUND OF
A SQUADRON OF
AIRCRAFT.

32. TITLE:
"The Absolute End."

Never Call Me at the Offus

Nowadays instead of cultivating the fields within hollering distance of hot biscuits for lunch, most men leave home to spend the day cultivating other people. The experts say this is bad for children, who no longer know what father does for a living.

Years ago they couldn't help knowing. He leaned on the fence and gave directions while the children hoed the corn, that's what. (If you ask me, child labor wasn't all bad.)

When today's children wave good-by to father in the morning, for all they know he could have burglar tools in his attaché case.

"Where's Daddy going, Mommy?"

"To the office."

"What's an off—offus?"

"It's where Daddy's job is."

"Why does Daddy have jobs?"

"It's like this, dear. We need money to go to the store to buy food and clothes and toys and gin. And our good Daddy goes out to work at his job every day to get the money for us."

From this conversation, heard with only slight variations in every house on the block, any normally intelligent child would conclude that Daddy is indeed a burglar—on his way to pull a job, just as Mommy said.

I don't want my children to grow up thinking their father is a burglar. When the question of father's occupation was raised at our house, I took pains to explain. I described for them what fathers do when they go downtown every day to work in their offices. It was easier for them to understand when I pointed out that what goes on at the office isn't much different from what goes on at school.

The children begin their school day with the Pledge of Allegiance. At the office, just turning up is a pledge of allegiance of sorts. Father's physical presence announces that when he resigned in a rage the previous night for the forty-third time, he really didn't mean anything by it. Especially since he didn't mention to anybody that he was quitting.

While the children are opening their books, the fathers are opening their mail. I always divide mine into three parts: letters asking me to subscribe to magazines I don't read, appeals to worthy causes I never heard of, and everything else. Two office boys then come in with wheelbarrows and cart the first two piles away to sell to the wastepaper dealer, which I am told is the main source of profit for many companies nowadays.

Next it is time for the morning coffee break, which parallels the school milk program. At school the children are scolded if they spill their milk. At the office someone always spills coffee somewhere so nothing much is made of it. A smart secretary will bring important letters and documents to her boss wrapped in clear plastic food bags. Then, when he starts splashing coffee and coffee-cake frosting in all directions, no serious damage results. Less foresighted secretaries have to type everything over again and hope they can get it mailed before the afternoon coffee break.

As the morning passes its prime, the school children reach the hour for Show and Tell. "Our new dog bit Daddy last night, and see, here's a piece of his new pants that was tored off."

There is also a Show and Tell time at the office. A customer has come in for a conference, and all the men important enough to have offices with windows have gathered round to show him something. It is a Chart. On the Chart are two wiggly lines. One line slants down toward the lower right-hand corner. That is bad. That line symbolizes the catastrophes that will overtake the customer's business if he continues doing things the same old way.

Don't feel sorry for him yet. There is another line. It rises toward the upper right-hand corner. It is the good line. It represents the sales increases the customer can expect if he heeds the advice being given him at that very moment.

The customer is impressed and signs his name on the contract. And they all live happily ever after—until some bad men whose office is around the corner show the customer another Chart and get him to sign *their* contract. They cheated, children; they had their Chart painted on a model's bare abdomen.

Lunch time. The children in school open their lunch boxes and take out their sandwiches. Their mothers have fixed just what they asked for, but they do not eat their own sandwiches. Instead, they trade lunches with other children and eat food they would not even slip to the dog at home. Downtown, all the fathers walk down the street to a restaurant called The Lunch Box. Although the food in The Lunch Box is generally considered inferior, martinis are only sixty cents before five o'clock, so naturally that's where everyone who works in the neighborhood eats. Or, rather, passes the lunch hour, which isn't necessarily the same.

In the afternoon, while the children take up their studies again, the fathers at the office resume such activities as practical psychology, the stalling bee, readings in contemporary sales literature, joke-ography and the expense account quiz, which Daddy had better not flunk unless he wants to be kept after class.

"See here, Baggit. I have a few questions about your last expense account."

"Yes, sir?"

"Why did you have to go to New York?"

"I had to see the department head at Apex to pick up the changes in their new contract."

"Couldn't you have got the information by mail? Or phone?"

"Well, his line was busy for a couple of days so I thought I'd better grab a plane and settle everything at once."

"Who is the department head at Apex now?"

"Bob Baggit."

"Same name as yours!"

"My brother, sir. Isn't that a coincidence?"

"Remarkable. Frankly, Baggit, I wonder why it was necessary to spend $300 on entertainment when the contract has already been approved by their top management and the department head is your own brother."

"The trouble isn't my brother, sir. It's his boss, the division vice president."

"Is he against the contract? Did he make you review the figures with him again?"

"No, sir. He thinks the contract is fine. But he sure likes to live it up. Would you believe it? A man in his sixties and he could almost keep up with Bob and me. Of course, he never made it to the last two or three spots. We poured him on his train first. But he made a splendid showing, considering his age."

"Baggit, Internal Revenue will never let us get away with entertainment expenses like these. You'll have to revise your expense account and make these items more reasonable. Don't leave yet."

"Sir?"

"Would you please tell me how your transportation expenses to New York and back could possibly be $2428."

"I'm sorry about that, sir. I left my copy of the contract on the plane and they flew it to London."

"What's that got to do with it?"

"I had to catch a plane to London to get my contract so I could be on time for my meeting with Apex. You know what sticklers for punctuality they are."

"Were you on time?"

"No trouble at all, sir. My brother Bob merely flew over to London where I was. The vice president didn't come because of his hangover. But I am sure Bob wasn't offended. You don't have to worry about that. I picked up his tab for everything."

"I know I've told you the company expects its representatives to project a favorable image, Baggit, but I think you've overdone it a bit. And how come this expense voucher totals up to $9386? Even if we allowed you the full amount on every item, the total would still be only $6328."

"It's the New Math, sir. I've had trouble with addition ever since I started helping the children with their homework."

Daddy is still slaving away at the office when the children arrive home from school. Distracted by the day's experiences, they have forgotten what they have been told about father's occupation.

"Where's Daddy? What's an off—offus? Why does he go there every day?"

On some occasions Mommy feels more harassed than usual. It is raining out and the furnace man, the appliance man and the plumber are tracking in mud and hammering on the walls.

"Daddy goes to the office every day, children, so he can get out of watching the baby while I take a nap."

Fire Me Again, Chief, It Feels So Nice

Critics are always analyzing the communications media and exposing the subtle forces that influence them. Depending on the investigator's point of view, we learn that Communist-sympathizer banjo players and fellow-traveling liberal news writers have infiltrated everywhere or that publishers, broadcasters and advertisers are conspiring with big business to brainwash the public.

The question deserves study. Only by being aware of the biases built into a publication or a television show can the public bring to bear the appropriate degree of skepticism.

Unfortunately, no one uncovered the real guiding spirit of press and broadcasting until I discovered that mass communications media in the United States are controlled by masochists.

I first suspected the truth when I saw an ad a few years ago placed by a well-known mass circulation magazine in newspapers read by potential advertisers. The ad boasted that the magazine staffers were so dedicated to their work that they held staff meetings at ten o'clock at night. This puzzled me. I could understand how editors, art directors, chief photographers and such— a notoriously disorganized crew—could find themselves scrambling around late at night trying to send the magazine to press. But I couldn't follow the publisher's reasoning in confessing this state of affairs to the public. Only when I began to detect the underlying note of masochism did I realize that some people aren't happy unless they have to work at ten o'clock at night.

With this clue to follow up, I began to study other evidence. One can learn much about any industry from reading the "Help Wanted" ads that appear in its trade journals. I was not disappointed by the ads I saw in *Advertising Age, Editor & Publisher, Publishers Weekly* and other journals in the communications field. They reeked of masochism.

"Help Wanted" ads are placed by employers because they wish to attract as many applicants as possible. Presumably, having advertised for personnel many times before, employers have learned by trial and error which appeals pull resumés from qualified applicants. The examples I collected show clearly that if an employer advertises a better masochist trap, a world of talent will beat a path to his door.

Here is the headline from an ad placed by an advertising agency that apparently had used up its masochists and needed a fresh supply. "Our best offer: a chance to fall on your face." The text of the ad warned, "We put plenty of responsibility on our new people. Some stagger a little. Others buckle at the knees. Then we try to shore them up, but we don't take the load off. After a while (with considerable effort on their part), they gradually learn to handle the job. *Then we usually add more work. . . ."*

The italics are mine. This statement is a key theme in a field where nothing is said about good pay, pleasant working conditions, fringe benefits or other advantages that would attract a normal person.

"Editor wanted with fire in his belly," advertised a publisher. "Write and tell us why you're the man to make this opportunity a lifelong career." This publisher obviously has reason to believe the country is full of editors who want a lifelong fire in the belly. (Doctors have another name for it. They call it an ulcer.)

One employer advertised for a man eager to work a seventy-hour week. Another wanted a man "so hooked on things creative that your work comes very close to being your total life." This is not to be confused with an LSD trip.

A newspaper paid for this ad:

"If there is such a person in existence who is willing to work on a county-seat weekly as a reporter, help keep the subscription list up to date, take classified ads, help out on display advertising on occasion, help the bookkeeper now and then, and still stay enthusiastic, bright and happy, we have a permanent opening."

This advertiser didn't say how many hours a week were required, but it has to add up to at least one hundred.

Besides baiting prospective staffers with a chance to work on the rock pile, employers in the communications field—like trout fishermen—know other ways to tie a fly. If applicants won't bite on just plain hard work, deadline pressure is waved in front of their noses. "You must thrive on a fast pace," said one ad. "We are a very fast track," said another, which went on to mention additional inducements: "The work is hard and challenging, the hours are long."

Taking off their coats at work is another irresistible attraction for masochists. The ads say: "We need a hard-working, shirt-sleeve editor" or "To the man we want we offer the chance to roll up his sleeves." This is especially mysterious. In any publication office I was ever in, the man who periodically came out of the corner office and whipped the slaves in shirt sleeves always had his coat on. The only job in the establishment better than his belonged to the man who sent in critical memos from the deck of his yacht in Florida. And he didn't have a coat to take off. He wasn't even wearing a shirt.

There seems no limit to the degree of maltreatment that will draw job seekers. "We might drive you nuts," said a Dallas advertising agency candidly. They added, cryptically, "You must want a Dallas salary." Possibly that means in the end they shoot you.

What is the normal person's response to propositions like these? Does he leap to leave a forty-hour-a-week job for one that takes seventy hours? Especially if it's fast-paced? And he has to work in his shirt sleeves? For a Dallas salary? I say he'd walk, not run, to the nearest hammock and lie down until all those masochistic offers went away.

A friend of mine suggested I was misinterpreting the evidence. He said these ads pull because the applicants already have jobs so miserable that the working conditions described sound like an improvement. Seventy hours a week is a sinecure if you're used to working eighty or ninety. I report this theory only in the interests of fairness. I don't believe it contradicts my discovery of the prevalence of masochism.

The fact is that jobs in newspaper and magazine offices, broadcasting studios and advertising agencies are being filled by the kind of men attracted by the chance to give their all, night and day while the boss rewrites their copy and lashes them with memos. This helps explain why certain attitudes are widespread in the mass media, which can't help reflecting the masochistic attitudes of the men who control them.

Consider the tendency of newspapers to attack public employees for loafing. There is a tradition in politics that the duties of certain positions in the lower levels of government shall not be onerous. This is to provide support for precinct captains and other essential servants of the party in power. They would be unable to serve the party nearly so well if they had to work full-time in industry. Kept within reasonable bounds, this tradition has never offended my tax-paying sensibilities. I consider it part of the cost of an effective two-party system, which the public has to pay for, one way or another. Nothing is free. The main trouble is that sometimes one party corners all the political jobs in a community. Then the precinct captains of the other party have to wear themselves out earning a living at a regular job. They are tired from working before the politicking even begins while their competition is fresh from a nap at City Hall. That doesn't seem fair.

Journalistic masochists, having created difficult hours and demanding deadlines for themselves, are envious of anyone who appears to be taking it easy. So a reporter and a photographer will conceal themselves for three days without food or water inside a garbage can to catch a truck crew of "payrollers" knocking off early to ring doorbells.

Some of the magazines—such as the ones devoted to travel and gracious living—are compelled by their formats and their advertisers to pretend they favor activities that cannot coexist with the seventy-hour week. Perhaps this is why there is an air of unreality about magazines like *Holiday* and *Sunset* and *House Beautiful*. Like the editors themselves, the more affluent members of society are grinding away at the "fast track." They don't have time to take leisurely trips to exotic faraway places or putter around with an exquisite Japanese garden.

"I found paradise on remote Breadfruit Atoll." The story tells how the author unwinds from the tensions of modern living by spending six weeks a year spearing fish and living in a palm-thatched hut on an island completely out of touch with civilization. The editor who supervised the story and arranged for the photographs hasn't been home on time for dinner since October, 1961.

On radio, the most popular kind of radio programming consists of ad-libbing disk jockeys who are on the air interminably. At least they seem interminable. When I glanced at the weekly log of a large network station that depends heavily on three well-known personalities, I found all of them work hours that cut them off from normal contact with family and friends. One of the "deejays" reports for work shortly after five A.M. six days a week. He must go to bed as early as a farmer. Another has no social life either because he nearly always works evenings. The one with the closest approximation to normal working hours is tied up at the station every Sunday all day.

You can't expect any of *them* to celebrate the anniversary of Thoreau's birth with a special broadcast on the superiority of a life dedicated to leisure and reflection, a life with "a broad margin."

As for television, the masochistic tendencies of *that* medium explain why the networks occasionally put on a high-quality show without much appeal to the masses. It is a painful experience for the executives as they take a beating in the ratings, but they are drawn to it—just as they are drawn to program the usual TV idiocy which offends their personal tastes. Born to suffer. Of course, the FCC hovering in the background has something to do with it, too. I can't blame masochism for everything.

After stumbling on my new insight into mass media and masochism, I thought I might write a book showing how all writers, artists and performers are basically masochists. Except me. Then I received a telephone call that put an end to the project.

"Frisbie? This is—well, I reckon y'all recognize the voice. Listen. We have a job for you down here in Washington."

"I'm flattered that you'd call me, sir, but I'm writing this book about—"

"Never mind the book, son. Let me tell you about this job. First, we work seven days a week."

"That IS challenging," I conceded. "What are the duties?"

"Mainly to answer the phone promptly when I call you up at night, say three or four A.M."

"I suppose I could think it over."

"Oh, you don't have to brood about it. You'll love it. I yell at you three or four times a week and the newspapers will criticize you every day."

I felt my resolution faltering.

"Nobody gets a vacation and someday, when you're in a tight corner and particularly need the money, your job will be abolished. And once you're out of government in Washington you're out of everything."

"What does it pay?"

"I'm surprised at you of all people asking a materialistic question like that. Sooner or later, the bank will foreclose your mortgage and some nationally syndicated columnist will attack your loyalty, your intelligence and your character coast to coast."

"Never mind the pay!" I shouted. "Never mind the duties! When do I start? I can't wait."

Some of My Best Friends Were Children

During one of the civil-rights debates in Washington, some members of Congress thought it would be a good idea to prohibit discrimination against families with children in the sale or rental of housing. "That's an outrage," complained a man who frequently sits next to me on the commuter train. He jabbed at the story in the newspaper with his finger so hard that it came out the other side like a circus dog jumping through a paper hoop. "I don't mind better conditions for children in some ways, but I'm not going to let the Government tell me I have to live next door to them. A man's home is his castle."

"What do you have against children?" I asked. While he wasn't looking, I quickly swallowed the photo of my eight children that I usually carry in my wallet. "In most cities, a call girl can rent any apartment her customers can afford while a respectable family is turned away time after time just because they have children. I don't understand it."

"Children run down a neighborhood in no time," he snapped. "They throw garbage out the windows. Any neighborhood that has children soon has apple cores and ice-cream-bar sticks and candy wrappers lying around all over the sidewalks. They break windows with balls. You see the ragged remains of their kites dangling from the utility poles.

"They take no pride in their housing. They'll nail a few boards together up in a tree and move in. Or they dig a hole in a vacant lot, put a few boards across it and call it their clubhouse. Who wants that sort of thing next door? I don't."

I said there were some good children. He didn't seem to hear me.

"Then there's the violence," he continued. "I know. I used to live in a neighborhood with children. I saw one case with my own eyes. There was a boy about three riding down the sidewalk on his tricycle. He had to stop because the sidewalk was blocked by a little girl with a doll buggy. I think she was his own sister. When he asked her to get out of the way, she whacked him over the head with the hard plastic doll, pushed him off the trike and rode away on it herself. A shocking case of armed assault, incipient auto theft, habitual criminality and interference with the mail."

"The mail?"

"Yeah. The boy was delivering birthday-party invitations."

I suggested it wasn't fair or logical to make generalizations from one isolated incident.

He paid no attention. "What's more, they attract each other. Let one in and before you know it, he has his friends over to play basketball—that's five on a side—or maybe even football. That can go as high as twenty-two for every game."

By then I was growing annoyed. "You're prejudiced," I said.

"Not prejudiced, just realistic. I suppose I wouldn't mind an

Eagle Scout here and there, but so many children are bubblegum addicts." He shuddered. "I've seen them. They get a wild
look in their eyes and stand around the streets in small groups
working their jaws all at once and trading cards."

"What's wrong with that?"

"That's the trouble with you bleeding-heart liberals—let anybody do anything. Bubblegum addicts leave the gum around
after they've chewed it. And you should see what that does to
a neighborhood.

"A fresh piece of well-chewed bubblegum will snatch the
shoes off a grown man quick as a wink. Little old ladies get
stuck in it and have to be rescued. I remember one time a fire
truck going to a fire struck a patch of bubblegum and it took
them three days to blast it loose."

I hoped he was running out of arguments so I could get
back to reading my newspaper, but he was only warming up. He
took a new tack.

"Children are filling up the schools," he said, somewhat louder
than before. "Once children start coming into a school it goes
one hundred per cent every time. No wonder they have trouble
getting teachers. If it weren't for all those children in every
classroom, teaching would be an attractive job. I'd go for it
myself. But what adult wants to lower himself by associating
with children all day? Depraved little things! I understand some
of them go in the coatroom and play doctor.

"And think how much lower the taxes would be if the schools
weren't full of children. We could build smaller schools and
make them pay their own way by renting them out nights as
telephone booths."

I objected. "But if we didn't send children to school, what
would become of them?"

"Oh, there's plenty for them to do with their time. Delivering newspapers, carrying golf clubs, mowing grass—"

I interrupted him. "How can you get your grass mowed if the
children don't live in your neighborhood?"

He ignored me. "If you're not careful, your daughter will

wind up marrying one. Teenage marriages are getting commoner every day. I say go slow."

"The trouble with gradualism," I countered, "is that by the time your type does anything about the problems of children, the children have grown up and become adults themselves. You can't just be against everything. You have to offer some constructive ideas."

By this time he was shouting. "I have a positive program. I say send them all back to Disneyland." He scooped up his paper and brief case, then moved to another seat at the far end of the car. You just can't talk to some people. (I suspect he has a touch of childish blood himself.)

When I returned home that night, I reported the conversation to the children, who were indignant. "Comes the revolution," said little Croakley, "we'll fix guys like that. We'll mount guitar amplifiers on motor scooters and blast them out of their holes."

"That's the wrong approach," said one of the girls. "They'll only get ear plugs and you'll be right back where you started. Croakley, you have to realize that violence only provokes a reaction."

The consensus among the children favored non-violence. Someone pointed out that Halloween was coming. "We'll have a massive demonstration. Instead of trick-or-treating in the adult neighborhoods, we'll stay home quietly and read uplifting literature—and they'll have to eat their own cheap candy for a change."

My son Marty cried, "Christmas!"

I asked what he meant.

"Christmas is when we'll really go after those prejudiced adults in our non-violent way. No cute letters to Santa Claus for them to read about in the papers. We won't go to the department stores to stand around and gape at the toys. We won't open our presents and say goody-goody. We'll spoil the holiday for them with a sulk-in, and it will serve them right."

I was proud of Marty. He's the thoughtful one. But he wasn't finished. "You know," he said to the other children, "they say that part of our problem, part of what makes us unacceptable to adult society is our inadequate family life. And I guess you know who's fault that is."

Suddenly they were all staring at me with cold eyes. There was only one thing to do. I took them all to the movies—making certain to stay clear of one that had a sign out front saying "ADULTS ONLY."

Paranoid's Guide to Current Events

In this era of ecumenism and improving interracial relationships, there is still one large group of Americans who have been left out of it all. I feel a special responsibility toward them because over the years I, as a writer and editor, have received so much mail from them. In fact, if it weren't for worthy causes, charge accounts and my faithful paranoid correspondents, I would receive hardly any mail at all.

We really ought to extend the arms of brotherhood to all of our fellow citizens who are being followed, stared at, conspired against, infiltrated or sprayed with secret rays by Them. The prejudice against this sensitive group—paranoids—is longstanding. History books never do justice to the contributions made by paranoids to the growth of our civilization. You probably have never read anywhere that the alphabet was invented by some Phoenicians who discovered that hieroglyphic writing was a code through which Egyptian secret agents were trying to corrupt the Phoenician public-school system.

The ancient city of Troy might not have fallen if the authorities had listened to Cassandra. She kept telling them there were Greeks in the woodwork, but with the usual anti-paranoid prejudice they dismissed her warnings lightly. I don't suppose we should be too critical of the Trojan authorities. They had to listen to a lot of nonsense in those days from kooks who thought they saw sphinxes and hydras and gorgons around every corner.

In Roman times, many of the best-remembered emperors were paranoids. In the classic paranoid style, they suffered from the conviction that someone wanted to kill them. A modern psychiatrist would have sent for the wagon.

"Doctor, you've got to help me."

"Yes, Phrivolus, lie down here on the couch and tell me all about it."

"I have this feeling that someone's trying to kill me."

"What makes you think that?"

"For one thing, the last eight slaves appointed to taste my food have all died within the week."

"Probably malaria, Phrivolus, what else?"

"There was an asp in my bed last night."

"Could have been a bad dream."

"And this morning the Praetorian Guard broke down the door and started throwing spears at me."

"Come now, Phrivolus, you're the Emperor. They wouldn't do that to you. . . . Phrivolus, speak to me . . . Nurse!"

"Yes, Doctor?"

"Call the police! The Praetorian Guard just came in and murdered the Emperor!"

As events proved, Roman emperors who thought someone was trying to kill them often had the last laugh on those who dismissed this fear as a delusion.

The Christian era introduced a new phase of paranoid thought. The discovery was made that the world was coming to an end any minute. That is, some paranoids favored the "any minute" theory. Others believed the teachings of the Saturnine school, which held that the world would come to an end next Saturday. Or, at worst, the following Saturday. Ever since, generation after generation has stayed up late on Saturday nights in order not to miss anything.

As is generally known, the event had not occurred as of this writing, although since I am typing this page on a Thursday morning I suppose there is still time before Sunday.

The worst problem for paranoids is not prejudice. They're used to that. What bothers them most today is the difficulty, in a world of rapid change, of knowing whom to blame for crop failures, setbacks in foreign affairs, the baseball standings, and volcanic eruptions. It used to be easier. During the middle of the nineteenth century, paranoids who happened to be native-born American Protestants could blame the Catholics. The Catholics could blame the Masons or (if Irish) the English. Later, at the peak of the drive to organize the unions, socialists could be discovered lurking in the background of every calamity.

In our own era, it was easy enough for a time to pin everything on the Communists, but in recent years considerable confusion arose as they split into two camps: the Good Communists and the Bad Communists. The Good Communists include the Poles, the Yugoslavs and the Russians. The Bad Communists are the Chinese, the Cubans and the Albanians. (Old Chinese saying: "People with stlange bedfellows toss in sleep. *Calamba!*"

A few of the older paranoids are still blaming Communists for tornadoes, Dutch Elm disease and pop/op art, but most realize the Communist era ended with the Second Vatican Council. Since no Communist could conceivably become a Catholic bishop and there obviously was some kind of sinister conspiracy behind the reforms in the liturgy, some new group must be running things now.

A number of my regular correspondents pointed out the significance in the increase of Unidentified Flying Object sightings since the end of the Council. But I received many other opinions, too. I compiled a list of frequently mentioned candidates for blame, which I offer here for its historical interest: Lyndon B. Johnson (Americans always blame the President for everything), Martin Luther King, Frank Sinatra, Leo Durocher, Leonard Bernstein, The Beatles, Batman and Robin, Cardinal Ottaviani, Pogo.

It happens that I myself am being slowly poisoned, but I do not blame anyone in the public eye. These were false leads. I have discovered that invaders from another planet, who have successfully infiltrated us disguised as earthmen, are to blame.

The truth began to come to me as I accumulated a record of their acts of sabotage against our planet. The air was being poisoned with fumes from cars and factories. Sewage, chemicals and old mattresses were being dumped into rivers. Various kinds of wildlife were being killed off.

Even the food was being sabotaged. Hepatitis in clams and oysters. Cancer on cranberries. Strange things happened to food on farms, and when it got to the store, it sat on the sidewalk in front of the supermarket and defrosted.

(The worst shock of all was to read that something they're feeding chickens causes arsenic to accumulate in chicken livers. The amount was said to be so small you'd have to eat a carload of chicken livers to feel any ill effects. That was no comfort to me, since I started on my second carload years ago.)

Scenery was bulldozed, paved or flooded by dams. Recreational land was buried under empty beer cans and highway cloverleaves.

I was sure all this was being done by invaders from outer space because no reasonable person would treat his own planet this way. Then I caught one of Them with incriminating evidence in its hand.

I was at a cocktail party. The Thing from outer space was there, too, disguised as a woman in a black dress. At first, I saw only an attractive woman helping the hostess by circulating the hors d'oeuvres. Then the Thing approached me, smiled a horrible smile and placed something in my hand. It was a cracker smeared with *chopped chicken liver!*

They must know I'm on to Them. That's why They're trying to kill me. I suppose They'll get me in the end, but if I ever have the chance I'm going to walk all over *Their* planet with the muddiest shoes I can find.

I've been passing on my discovery to as many of my paranoid friends as I can reach. Many of them suspected it all the time. There has been one beneficial result. Now that we know we can blame everything on invaders from outer space, we can release all our terrestrial scapegoats. Good thing, too, because they've been eating us out of house and home.

The Better Part of Wisdom

I've told the children they have no reason to act smart just because I can't help them with the New Math. Modern science is only beginning to find proof for many things I have always known. To convince them of this fact, I began to keep a scrapbook of newspaper clippings. The first entry was this one:

> Recent psychiatric studies at the University of Michigan indicate that more than half the drivers responsible for a series of fatal automobile accidents suffered from some form of mental illness.

In other words, if the inherently unsafe design of your car doesn't kill you first, you are likely to be picked off by some nut. Fortunately, having been born knowing this, I long ago devised a diagnostic method for telling which other drivers on the road are mentally unbalanced (all of them) and sorting them into categories.

The classic paranoid driver thinks all the other drivers have conspired to block his path and prevent him from reaching his destination. My basic test is to delay a few seconds in starting up when the traffic light changes to green. The paranoid behind will honk his horn every time.

A more sophisticated test for paranoia is to drive a few miles an hour slower than the posted speed limit. When you do this, you'll observe that car after car speeds past you while the drivers honk and work their mouths behind their car windows, presumably screaming imprecations at you for not driving faster. I have concluded that paranoid drivers are exceedingly common.

The diagnostic test for schizophrenia requires a foggy night in the country. Under these circumstances, schizophrenic drivers often lapse into catatonic trances and continue racing along the highway as if they were driving in clear daylight. I believe some of them imagine themselves to be projectiles that have been fired at the moon. All of them obviously imagine that they can see where they are going.

There is a somewhat diffuse type of mental imbalance that gives drivers a compulsion to fill up empty spaces in traffic. Test procedure: in heavy traffic slow down to leave double the recommended safe distance between you and the car in front of you. Compulsives can't bear it. They'll swerve in to cut you off whenever they can. I have observed many dramatic examples. One compulsive chased me at a speed of at least 200 miles per hour in order to cut me off. Several habitually hide in country lanes until they see a tempting opening in front of my car. An unfortunate case tried to swerve across three lanes of a throughway to fill up the opening in front of me, but he was picked off by a paranoid in a large truck.

The worst kind are the manic-depressives because they often have suicidal tendencies. They pass on hills and curves, drive in the dark without lights and suddenly change lanes or stop for no apparent reason. Too many of them not only want to go ahead of schedule; they want to take you with them. The only defense is to drive the way experienced pilots fly; instead of always having a possible crash-landing site in view, you keep your eyes open for the softer ditches with no concrete culverts in them.

Suppose you encounter a mishap in one of your driver diagnostic tests and have to go to a hospital. Here's another item in my news scrapbook:

A study of medication errors in hospitals showed they were occurring at the rate of at least every sixth dose.

I knew it, I knew it. They have been trying to get rid of me for years. That's why, whenever I have been sick, I have contrived to pour any medicine offered me into the nearest flowerpot. Now that the truth is out, I'm glad I did. However, I have suffered a few pangs of conscience over the plants in the pots. Most of them died.

The lower animals, with their senses unblunted by alcohol and garlicky cooking, protect themselves by instinct from being dosed with the wrong medicine. Or any medicine. I once tried for three days to get our dog to take a pill. I hid it in chicken livers, mashed it up in gravy and tried to poke it down her gullet from the corner of her mouth, as the vet recommended. She would patiently endure all, then spit it out under the dining-room radiator at the first opportunity.

Now that my suspicions have been confirmed, I know exactly what to do the next time I'm sick. If I'm served chicken livers, I'll slip every sixth one to the dog.

News item:

Memory becomes less efficient with age, a Canadian psychologist reported as a result of an experiment with words.

I suppose it's useful to have these facts nailed down experimentally, although, as I have explained, they are no surprise to me. Otherwise, I'd have to concede it is at least theoretically possible that I'm the only person whose memory is slipping with increasing age.

Just the other day I forgot entirely to answer a letter from a Catholic organization. I found it today under a pile of papers. Such a polite letter, too. The last paragraph said:

I regret we are unable to offer an honorarium, furnish transportation, or provide any other expenses for our speakers. All we can offer you is the knowledge that your words will have a significant impact on many.

When I was younger, I would have remembered to answer a polite letter like that (despite the fact that I knew the sponsoring organization was paying the going rate for meeting space in a first-class hotel). But now that I'm older, it slipped my mind entirely. What's the word I'm trying to think of? Oh, yes. Alas.

What Can You Expect from Slickers Who Wore Knickers?

While I was pondering whether to write about the brilliant new solution to the Vietnam problem that came to me recently in the shower or to set forth a crystal-clear analysis of current trends in theology (derived from seventeen years I once spent meditating on a salt pillar), I realized I had something in common with the men now reaching the age to take over key positions in our institutions of power—government, business, press, education, church. We passed together through a unique experience in our formative years, an experience certain to affect the quality of our century.

We all wore knickers.

They were strangely impractical garments. Because the elastic cuff was made tight enough to grip your leg just below the knee, you couldn't take them off or put them on while wearing your shoes. This made parental regulations about taking off school knickers and putting on old knickers before going out to play difficult to enforce.

Some boys consistently came out to play in their school knickers, which obviously was one of the sources of the lack of respect for authority so rampant today. Others, having proceeded only as far as taking off their shoes, became absorbed in an after-school radio serial or similar indoor pastime, whence stems the nation's decline in physical fitness.

Knickers could be a guide to personality. There was a tidy, born-to-keep-the-books type of boy who always wore his knickers properly, with elastic cuff just below the knee and long stockings pulled up straight and tight. Sister despaired of the disorganized, sloppy boys who came to school with knickers bagging down on top of stockings that had sagged into loose, woolly spats. She feared those boys would come to a bad end. She was right. I know because I was one of them.

Also, there were boys who wore one leg up and the other down. These were the adaptable personalities who grew up to fit in so well with the demands of modern superorganizations.

In my neighborhood it wasn't easy to keep your knickers on. The boys practiced a custom called "pantsing." A group of young ruffians would ambush another boy, hold him down, yank off his knickers and throw them over the fence into someone's yard. This fate could overtake a boy because (1) he was popular or (2) he was unpopular.

(This was more charitable than what happened to one of my fraternity brothers at the University of Arizona. In that instance, the boys kept the pants and threw HIM over the wall into a sorority's patio.)

When a popular boy was "pantsed," it was because his peer group wished to bestow on him a mark of their favor. When an unpopular boy was "pantsed," it was a sort of symbolic lynching. I was never sure what they meant by it, but when my own knickers started up the flagpole at school I did feel that my classmates had hostile motives.

"Pantsing" victims always resisted strenuously. It was quite a challenge to pull off the elastic cuffs of knickers over a healthy boy's kicking feet. This may explain why "pantsing" was so popular during the heyday of knickers and died out later when baggy trousers made it too easy.

When today's middle-aged sociologist writes movingly of the problems of alienation, he is subconsciously recalling how it felt to be "pantsed" after school on a November day, how rough and cold the tree bark felt on his bare knees and thighs as he shinnied up the trunk to haul down his knickers.

Knickers had their advantages. No finer escape-proof snake container has ever been invented. If you happened to catch a garter snake on the way to school, you *could* put it in your pocket. The snake *might* be content to stay put. More likely, he'd slip out in the middle of class, spreading consternation among the girls and earning you a week's sentence on the after-school rock pile under the unblinking eye of Sister M. Warden.

When wearing knickers, you could merely pull out your waist band and drop in your snake. He'd be snug and safe in your knickers for hours. Then, when you wanted to play with him after school, you just tugged on the elastic cuff, and out he dropped like a candy bar being delivered by a vending machine.

Knickers also saved you from property loss. At the time, you frequently found yourself with holes in your pockets, resulting from their use in the transportation of mineral specimens and other heavy objects. Fortunately, as your rosary, your Boy Scout knife and your money fell through the holes in your pockets your faithful knickers collected everything.

No doubt, having a mixed bag of snakes, knives, rosaries, coins and other objects rattling around your knees was a traumatic experience of some kind. My own recollection is casual enough, but that may be only on the surface. You can never be sure what repressed emotions are seething deep in the subconscious.

Suppose you pulled out your elastic cuff in the joyful expectation that sixteen cents for a milk shake would drop into your hand. Instead, you received a broken yo-yo, a crumpled bird's nest or some other useless object you had forgotten was there. Wouldn't that have an effect on your impressionable young mind, if not modifying your understanding of Providence, at least encouraging you in the future to play it cool? Today's society is shot through with a reluctance to be enthusiastic,

obviously resulting from the unpredictability of shaking out
knickers.

The reason knickers disappeared was that they wasted too
much cloth. With the advent of World War II and its material
shortages, the government discovered that the cloth from half a
dozen full-cut knickers could be put to better use as tents
for a platoon of infantry. (Soldiers on bivouac reported that
for some reason tents of this material seemed to attract snakes.)

When the end came, knickers had already done their damage.
They had subtly infected a whole generation with a wasteful
attitude toward national resources, which we now see expressed
in flagrant disregard of our cherished traditions of conservation.
The connection between having worn knickers and wanting to
flood the Grand Canyon with a new dam is easy to trace.

Keeping this background in mind helps me to see contemporary events in perspective. Whenever I have difficulty understanding the public position taken by another survivor of the
Knicker Era, I go home, make sure no one is looking and pull
on a pair of knickers that I had made for me secretly by a
CIA agent in Hong Kong who moonlights as a tailor. With
acres of fabric drooping from my belt like a furled main-
sail and the familiar squeeze of elastic cuffs on my calves, I
nearly always find myself able to understand the workings of
the rascal's mind perfectly. If, on occasion, this fails me, I
have merely to take my knickers off. Standing there knicker-
less, I can see clear to the bottom of a politician's soul.

When Willys-Knighthood Was in Flower

Anyone old enough to have spent his formative years as a
member of the medieval Church probably can remember when
driving around in an automobile on Sunday afternoon was still

considered a pleasure. A generation later that seems astonishing. Traffic was nearly as congested then as now, and driving conditions were primitive.

The narrow highways had a disconcerting tendency to make ninety-degree turns without being banked. After a summer weekend many a farmer awoke on Monday morning to discover a strange La Salle or Essex in his barn that had come in without permission through the wall facing the highway.

Highway planners have always been a notoriously cretinous lot. Now they think the best place for a cloverleaf is in a stand of redwood trees or on top of a historic building. Back in the thirties they thought they had made a great breakthrough in the development of transportation by inventing the three-lane highway. It probably killed more people than the Black Death.

"Here's the problem, sir. There are still numbers of motorists who believe that driving faster than a horse trot is flying in the face of Providence. Put a couple of them going in opposite directions on a standard two-lane highway and the traffic backs up for miles, especially on Sunday. All we have to do is widen the road one lane and the problem is solved. Faster traffic can take turns using a passing lane in the center. And even the classic road hog can't obstruct all three lanes unless he's driving a house mover's rig."

It sounded logical enough in theory, but in practice it didn't work out. Everybody drove in the center lane all the time—speed fiends, drunks, road hogs, little old ladies with electrics and farmers with tractors. The result was carnage.

But the public merely turned on the windshield wipers to clear off the blood spatters and continued on its way.

A popular destination on a summer Sunday afternoon was the fund-raising picnic at a country parish. Some Catholics subscribed to the diocesan weekly for the sole purpose of following the announcements of parish picnics. When they saw one listed, they'd drive for hours to get there.

The basics of a parish picnic were always the same. Under

one awning was the bar where the men spent the afternoon—
once the jousting and longbow shoot were over—with a copious
supply of beer and flies. The flies came after some of the
beer had been spilled on the planks forming the temporary bar
and warmed by the hot sun to a fragance of such irresistible and
nutritious force it would resurrect flies who had already died.

Under another awning was the gambling house. Minimum
attractions were bingo and a raffle. The more enterprising
parishes might run a dice game besides. Among the patrons
were regulars who followed the parish picnic circuit Sunday
after Sunday.

I remember these events as boring for a child. Even when
there were pony rides the excitement of jolting a couple of times
around the ring while a bad-tempered animal tried to bite my
foot seemed but a fleeting part of a long hot day. I greatly pre-
ferred those Sunday afternoon rides which wound up at a beach.
Many of them did. You can't drive hour after hour even in the
Midwest without eventually coming to water.

From our base on the South Side of Chicago we often
visited lakes in Wisconsin or the lakeshore duneland in Michigan. Illinois and Indiana, for the most part, were considered
too close to be worth the trouble of backing the car out of the
garage.

There was one exception: Indiana at that time was as full
of slot machines as Nevada is today. Many Chicagoans scheduled a gas stop in Indiana while en route to some more challenging destination so they could try for the jackpot. I liked
slot machines better than bingo myself. Bingo impressed me as
a way to get nothing for something, but with the slot machines
I got to watch the cherries, grapes and bell fruits whiz around
for my nickel.

When our destination was the water's edge, the food came
in a picnic case containing neatly fitted vacuum bottles and
sandwich boxes. The sandwich boxes were smaller in cross section than any loaf of bread ever sold, so the sandwiches had to
be cut down to size after they were made. This wasted about

a third of each sandwich. A child must somehow have influenced the design of the sandwich boxes because they automatically eliminated all crusts. Or maybe it was the Bread-and-Butter Interests encouraging waste as a stimulus to sales. I have noticed that such sandwich boxes in picnic kits are still being made too small today.

Sometimes on a Sunday my grandmother would announce that she felt like going out to dinner. Since she had infinite endurance for riding in a car, the restaurant she had in mind could be anywhere from Ohio to Iowa. I enjoyed these expeditions, pointless as they were. No matter how much I ate at The Old Spinning Wheel or the Whitefish Inn, by the time we reached home hundreds of miles later I was hungry again. Hungrier than usual, in fact, because of the well-known effect of fresh air.

These long rides posed for a child the problem of entertaining himself at length in a confined space. I could not read because the swaying of the car would make me sick if I tried. A rule against reading was enforced by the authorities, who didn't want to take unnecessary risks. Bringing toys along had limitations; my erector set kept falling over at curves. Part of the journey I would look at the scenery, read the billboards and try to outguess Burma-Shave on their own punch lines.

The most durable pastime was conducting experiments in aerodynamics. I made paper airplanes in various shapes and trailed them out the rear window on a string. None lasted long. If I kept the string short, the plane soon hammered itself to shreds on the car at sixty miles per hour. Lengthening the string meant the plane would be destroyed by the car following. Cars in those days had hood ornaments, and the bowsprit of a Plymouth ship or the horns of a Dodge ram would impale a paper airplane viciously. The solution was to bring plenty of paper and keep the aircraft factory producing. This had the additional advantage of providing a trail of torn paper to follow home if we lost our way in the woods.

I think cars on the road were more varied then than now,

representing more automotive generations. Lined up at a traffic
light you might see a couple of new Fords and Chevies not
much different from today's models except for styling and
lack of automatic transmission; a Model T, chattering and
vibrating; several Model A's with their tickety-tickety engines;
a Hudson Terraplane; a Lincoln roadster, with seats for only
two and an enormous engine on a chassis that seemed thirty
feet long; and three or four different kinds of the big square
sedans surviving from the late twenties.

One of these might be our neighbor's Willys-Knight. This
car was said to have been built of armor plate that became surplus when the Navy started scrapping battleships after the
Washington disarmament conference of 1922. I wouldn't be
surprised if it were bulletproof, although Mr. Fisher worked
at a respectable occupation and never had occasion to find out.

When you rap on the fenders of a modern car, you hear a
"tink, tink" sound, as if it were a washing machine or a fishing-
tackle box. If you rap hard, you'll make a dent. Good-by $114.73.
Rapping on the fenders of Mr. Fisher's Willys-Knight produced
almost no effect. It was like rapping on a steel bridge or a bank
vault. You couldn't have dented it with a brick.

The automobile industry counters the claim "they don't
build 'em like they used to" by pointing to the superiorities
of today's steels, which are said to be more resilient, safer and
more economical in the long run, easier to repair, blah, blah,
blah. But Mr. Fisher's Willys-Knight had an advantage no
manufacturer today could claim: its armor plate fenders sliced
up lesser cars like cheese.

Mr. Fisher cherished this quality of his car, although he was
not a reckless driver in the usual sense. He didn't speed or try
to pass everybody on the road or plunge around corners without
looking. What distinguished his wheelsmanship was his precise
concern for his rights.

One Thursday he was taking his wife to the fish store and
had just found a parking place directly in front when a smart
aleck in a newer and smaller car tried to dive into the parking

space behind him. Mr. Fisher pretended not to see. Slowly, inexorably, he kept backing up. There were frantic horn beeps—too late. The old Willys-Knight's rear bumper and right rear fender ripped off the left front fender and headlight of the other car and pried off the driver's door like a bottle cap. Damage to the Willys-Knight consisted of some severe paint scratches, no problem to Mr. Fisher since he painted it a new color every spring anyway. With house paint.

Another day, he was sitting patiently in a traffic jam at an intersection, waiting his turn to drive through a four-way stop. A newer car came bouncing along the shoulder of the highway from far to the rear of the line and tried to cut into the intersection in front of him. Mr. Fisher, seeing that it was his turn to go, went. His right front fender peeled off the hood and radiator of the other car and crunched the fragments against the stop sign post. The occupants of the other car were so indignant that Mr. Fisher for once forbore to linger and lecture them on driving courtesy.

Mr. Fisher, I think, cherished a secret wish to reform the driving habits of the nation. Given more time he might have achieved more influence. (Perhaps I should have said "impact.") Unfortunately, his career as a reformer was cut short.

One dark rainy night coming home from a church picnic, he turned into the center lane to pass a slower car on a three-lane highway. As he recalled later, he was in a cheerful mood. It was cozy driving in the rain in the Willys-Knight with the raindrops going plonk-plonk on the armor plate. He saw a car coming toward him with bright lights on. The driver seemed to have no intention of dimming them. Mr. Fisher flicked his own lights a couple of times. Still the two bright lights sped closer, as unblinking as twin comets.

"Reckless maniac," Mr. Fisher muttered. "I'll show him." Mr. Fisher flipped on his own brights and bore down on the gas pedal. The oncoming car neither dimmed its lights nor slowed down nor turned one inch out of the passing lane. Suddenly, Mr. Fisher screamed: "Dammit, Gloria, it's another Willys-Knight!"

Farmers in the area talked about the crash for years. The vibration derailed a freight train. A nearby creek flowed backwards and flooded 300 acres of corn. The sky rained auto parts for a week. When the scrap metal from the two wrecked cars was cleaned up, it was sold to Japan to help build a heavy cruiser.

Although Mr. Fisher, like the other victims, survived his injuries, his spirit was broken. When he finally bought a new car, it was a sporty little coupé, completely unsuited for combat. It even had a radio, sensitive to shock, and white sidewall tires, which needed protection from scuffing.

More Garlic than Phallic

Is American society really obsessed with sex? There seems to be considerable support for the argument that it is. One hears so much about it in sermons and editorials that a person who leads a quiet life can almost become persuaded he's missing something.

Many novelists and dramatists, acting on the assumption that the usual evaluation of our times is correct, fill their works with references to sex in all the usual varieties plus some new ones folks never heard of in Iowa City. Social critics say even our consumer goods are designed as phallic symbols. The explanation is that people like to be reminded of sex by books and egg beaters because in their personal sex lives they feel deprived and frustrated.

As far as I know, I am the first to notice the contradictions in this position.

A higher percentage of the population is married now than

at any other time in our history. (Teenage marriages are increasingly common, and ninety-three per cent of all American women still in their thirties have had at least one husband.) Presumably these couples do not spend all their time watching television. As for the unmarried, if we are to believe the moralists, writers and social critics, a great many people are having more sexual experience than is good for them. So why would they want to waste time reading about it? One way or another, people have little reason to be interested in vicarious sex.

There is, however, another basic human need that under present conditions could very well give people obsessions.

Food.

Outside the religious life, one doesn't meet many voluntary celibates. Most widows, widowers, spinsters and bachelors wouldn't mind a change in their luck. But nearly every adult man and woman in the country is on some kind of diet, trying to lose weight.

Once I realized that what most Americans are deprived of is not sex but satisfying high-calorie cooking, I began to see that the artifacts of our culture reflect culinary images at every turn. American society is more garlic than phallic.

Consider the dominant product in the nation's economy: the automobile. Much has been made over the years of the allegedly phallic connotations of various design elements, from the masculine projections of radiator ornaments to the soft curves of fenders, front and rear.

But, in the automobile trade, what term do you suppose is used to describe a desirable late model used car in excellent condition? "Sweetheart?" "Lover?" "Playmate?" "Toots?" "Broad?" Nope.

The answer is "Creampuff."

The deeper meanings of this usage are obvious enough. A creampuff is a highly caloric dessert no rational person dares eat as often as he'd like because he knows he's better off to spend his calories virtuously on high-protein foods with good amino acid balance and vitamin-packed (ugh!) vegetables. Similarly, a car buyer often would be more sensible to buy an economy model that's brand new than to spend as much or more money for a de luxe "creampuff" loaded with accessories to get out of order.

When Detroit first crossed the sedan with the convertible and bred the hardtop, an attempt was made to explain the immediate popularity of the hardtop in sexual terms. The convertible was said to symbolize a mistress—desirable but sinful. A hardtop was enough like a convertible to be desirable and enough like a sedan to assuage the male buyer's built feelings. But what was said of the man who bought a hardtop? "He's having his *cake* and eating it, too."

We are not always rational when our mouths are watering for a creampuff. We long to eat one kind, diet be damned, and buy the other, budget be blowed. But sex has nothing to do with it.

Glancing around at household objects, one readily discovers numerous examples of gastronomic symbolism. A sex-oriented critic might try to find libidinous meanings in a certain lamp with a breast-like contour. Actually, it looks like a mushroom being sautéed in an ocean of fresh butter. Or like a delicately poached egg, about to be served with ham, fried potatoes, hot cocoa and blueberry muffins.

The classic living-room chair design is a vertical stuffed lamb chop. Piano legs plainly were inspired by a plump chicken drumstick smothered in white gravy. In the kitchen, the toaster is an upsidedown cake and the counter tops are available in a delicious choice of colors—ice cream white, lemon cream pie green, chocolate cake brown, chicken curry yellow and blue stroganoff. The colors have other names in the catalogue, but their true food spirit comes through to the consumer.

I don't have facilities for conducting psychological field studies. However, there is always much to be learned from an examination of literature. To test my theory about the prevalence of food images, I pulled down an armload of contemporary books from my shelves at random and started from the beginning of each, looking for food references. I was surprised myself to see how food overwhelms sex as an all-pervasive theme.

Open the cover of *The Medium is the Massage* by Marshall McLuhan and Quentin Fiore, and what do you see? A picture on the very first page of an egg that appears to have been fried lovingly in butter.

James Baldwin could get only 104 words into *Go Tell It on the Mountain* before using a food word. The 105th word of the book is "breakfast." This same word appears in the twentieth line of *The Injustice Collectors* by Louis Auchincloss.

Rumer Godden mentions "olive" as the eighty-fourth word of *The Battle of the Villa Fiorita*. William Faulkner writes "smokehouse" as the third word and "drank" as the ninety-seventh of his 1938 novel *The Unvanquished*. Katherine Anne Porter is only in the second paragraph of *Ship of Fools* when she's talking about a "feast," and "lavish" at that.

In *The Wapshot Scandal*, John Cheever includes considerable incident of a non-edifying sort, but the first thing that happens in the whole book is the singing of a song by a railroad stationmaster: "Oh, who put the overalls in Mrs. Murphy's *chowder?*"

J. D. Salinger is still on the first page of *Raise High the Roof Beam, Carpenters* when he has the infant Franny Glass crying for her bottle. John O'Hara's fictional character, Howard Ambrie, begins the second paragraph of *The Cape Cod Lighter* by having a glass of milk and a piece of sponge cake.

The Stranger, by Albert Camus, opens with a telegram about the death of the protagonist's mother, but before the middle of the second page he is lunching "as usual" at Céleste's restaurant.

As for the great Hemingway, he wrote a book with food right in the title—*A Moveable Feast*. It opens in a café.

Even Erich Fromm, who writes philosophical and abstract non-fiction, uses "starved" as the eleventh verb in Chapter 1 of *The Art of Loving*.

I'm sure similar results would have been reached with any

other armload of current books. Authors are accused of having their minds in the bedroom; actually, their minds are in the kitchen, frying doughnuts in deep fat.

The same influence also governs the other arts. Painting? The traditional still-life usually depicts food—a bottle of wine, a loaf of bread and a couple of potatoes. The only reason the artist didn't paint a cream-cheese cake was that he couldn't afford one.

One whole school of contemporary abstractionists paints WITH food—scrambled eggs and Hungarian goulash with a dash of paprika for color. The pop-art fad was launched by paintings of soup cans. I must confess I find no food symbolism in the op art I have seen, but looking at the whirling circles and squares is so strenuous that visiting an exhibit always makes me hungry.

I have heard new music suggesting the sizzling of lobster tails broiling against a counterpoint of champagne bubbles. Contemporary sculpture has acquired a flowing free form suggestive of dumplings before they're dropped in with the chicken. In textiles what looks like the place where someone dropped the gravy boat is actually part of the pattern.

In the theater, a restaurant kitchen was recently moved to a stage in New York City and a professional short-order cook played four weeks off Broadway in a food happening. The critics said the ample action made up for a paucity of plot; the play smelled but it smelled good.

Although there is a strain of austerity in modern architectural styles, churches—including a certain national shrine—are still going up that can best be described as a double hot-fudge sundae with a maraschino cherry on top. Chicago's Marina City towers are widely known for their resemblance to ears of sweet corn, ready to be spread with butter and salt. Many new offices and apartments everywhere appear to have been copied from a club sandwich or a chocolate *torte*.

If you gave the average American the ink blot test, he'd be reminded of swirls of whipped cream every time.

The Man in the Ironic Masque

I found out about Herman's Acting School one night at a
party when I asked a pleasant young man what he did. He said
he was enrolled with Herman, studying a role. Not a play.
At Herman's Acting School they don't have plays, only roles.

He explained that Herman has finally liberated the drama
from its artificial setting in the theater and brought it out
into the fresh air and sunlight of life itself. Instead of sub-
jecting actors to the tyranny of one play script after another,
Herman coaches his students in selected lifelong roles as well
as certain temporary ones.

Naturally I was curious. So the next day I tracked down
Herman himself to learn more about his original theories.
Alighting from a taxi at the address I had been given, I noted
that Herman was a versatile entrepreneur. On the ground floor
of the building was a saloon identified by a sign as HERMAN'S
FIRST AID STATION. On the second floor other signs
painted on the windows advertised HERMAN'S ACTING
SCHOOL and HERMAN'S ACTORS' AGENCY.

The First Aid Station was ministering to a lively afternoon
trade, apparently composed largely of the thirsty members of
an expedition just returned to civilization after months in a
desert. I assumed that the bartender in charge of the cash
register would be Herman, but I was wrong.

"Herman don't work down here much any more," the bartender said. "He's too busy upstairs." He pointed to a stair-
case in the back. As I started up the stairs, he called after
me, "If you're the Rising-Young-Executive-Headed-for-the-Top,
you're behind schedule." I paused in surprise and opened my
mouth to ask him how he knew that. Then a door at the top

of the stairs opened and a man shouted, "I forgot to tell you, Joe, the Rising-Young-Executive-Headed-for-the-Top has already been up."

Mystified by this exchange, I stood stupidly on the stairs. The man on the second floor saw my confusion and introduced himself. "I'm Herman. If you haven't been here before, you may find the uproar around here a bit peculiar, but it can all be explained."

"That's why I came," I said. I told him about the young man at the party and his interesting account of the school. Herman was pleased. He said the young man had described the school well.

Herman, genial in an intense way, fortyish, talked freely. He said he had started the Acting School after years of running the First Aid Station because he had grown weary of listening to amateur role players at the bar night after night. He had decided to dedicate himself to increasing the world's supply of role players with professional training and skill.

Most of Herman's students were content to become proficient at stock roles like the Man-Who'd-Have-Made-a-Killing-If-He'd-Had-the-Breaks or She'd-Given-Her-Husband-the-Best-Years-of-Her-Life-and-Now-Look-at-the-Ungrateful-Slob. A few of the abler and more ambitious students persevered until they learned several roles.

This led to the establishment of Herman's Actors' Agency. There proved to be a steady demand for Herman's graduates to personify abstractions whenever contemporary problems were being seriously discussed. Herman's offbeat genius provided a practical concept—a team of actors trained to be the perfect archetypes.

For instance, the civil-rights team included a Southern Sheriff, an Outside Agitator, a White Northern Liberal, a Press Photographer and a Police Dog (which is played by a Labrador retriever who trained to be an understudy for Lassie but couldn't hold the job).

Herman's pacifism group employs a cast of three. One is the

Guy-with-a-Club, who symbolizes aggressor nations. The second actor, who shaves his head bare and paints a target on it, is the Victim. The third actor is the Bystander, representing the nations that have to decide what course of action to follow when confronted with the use of force.

"This group is especially interesting," Herman said, "because the actors can play it so many different ways. For a pacifist audience, the Victim just stands there and takes it until the club is smashed to splinters. For an audience of romantics the Bystander can do a St.-George-to-the-Rescue bit. If the audience is cynical, the Bystander will side with the Guy-with-a-Club and hold the Victim's arms."

For economics discussions Herman's group works around the common assertion that, if all the money in the world could be divided up evenly, at the end of ninety days the same persons would have it all back again. Herman provides a Man-Who-Gets-It-Back, a Man-Who-Can't-Hang-onto-His-Share and an Umpire. The Umpire's task is to prevent the others from going too far with their ad-libbing. In Herman's earliest productions on this theme too many aberrations cropped up. Sometimes the man who was supposed to get it back said he was glad to be rid of it. Or the man who was supposed to lose his share would stick to it like epoxy adhesive. These variations on the theme spoiled the show for many audiences who expected the action to follow the classical pattern, like a Japanese No Drama.

Only two roles are needed for urban renewal: the Immovable Object and the Irresistible Force. The Immovable Object argues movingly about the need to preserve communities, especially the one he lives in. The Irresistible Force counters with arguments for progress, pointing out that the Immovable Object lives in an unsanitary slum which ought to be torn down before it falls down. The Object retorts that the Force's new super-highway is just a traffic jam looking for a place to start and the Force's new housing projects will be worse than the slums they replace because buildings do not make a community. Like the pacifism discussion, this one turns out in various ways, depending on the audience. The most popular version winds up with a compromise: both sides agree to tear down the whole city and start over from the beginning.

The closest Herman and his actors come to melodrama is a group that performs for poverty discussions. The leading character is a mother on welfare with two illegitimate children. To satisfy audiences of all kinds, one of the children becomes a criminal. The other, Bright Slum Kid, meets Dedicated Teacher and earns a college scholarship. Bright Slum Kid goes on to become a doctor, specializes in research and discovers cures for cancer, heart trouble and the common cold.

In the field of religious drama, there is a team consisting of Reactionary Prelate, Zealous Young Priest, Emerging Layman and Apathetic Majority. They all cooperate in revitalizing the Church. Herman's catalogue lists this one as a "miracle play."

Herman said the Acting School is always at work developing new roles to meet popular demand.

I asked whether the actors tire of playing the same roles all the time.

Herman opened a drawer in one of the filing cabinets that lined his office. He took out a folder bearing the name of the young man I had met at the party.

"We are careful about matching the man and the role," Herman said. "This is our dossier on the actor who always plays the Negro-You-Wouldn't-Want-Your-Sister-to-Marry. He was Phi Beta Kappa at Michigan State, quite an athlete, a war hero—holds the Distinguished Service Cross—graduated first in his class at law school and is quite wealthy, thanks to an inheritance from an uncle who owned a farm smack in the middle of a big oil field in Texas. And he's Swedish."

"But that's absurd," I exclaimed.

"I'm glad you dig it," Herman said happily. "Most people require more explanation."

Stitches in Time

Not having seen as much of the world as I would like, I find it annoying to be trapped at parties by world travelers. Listening to them exchanging anecdotes about little restaurants in Paris or the shops in Hong Kong wearies me exceedingly. I have burned to counter with stories about my own travels in Time rather than Space, but I have taken my conversational lumps and held my peace.

Now I think the world is ready to know the truth about Time travel. In any case, I want my children to know of their father's adventures with the Time machine, and as soon as I tell them the word will get out anyway.

I stumbled on the facts about Time travel many years ago when I was a young newspaper reporter. I had been sent to interview a famous scientist about a new development in his field. After I had taken sufficient notes for my story, he invited me to tour his laboratory, which consisted of a number of small work rooms housed in a sprawling one-story building.

Midway in the tour, he was called to the telephone. He excused himself and left me standing in a corridor. When he didn't return in a reasonable time, I decided to find my own way back to the entrance, leave him a note and return to the paper to write the story.

I immediately blundered through the wrong door and found myself in a room that had not been part of the tour. For obvious reasons. Some experiment had miscarried and the room was a mess.

Equipment and books from the shelves lining the walls were spilled onto the floor. Several expensive-looking gauges were smashed. In one corner stood a large electronic machine with a compartment at one end similar to the take-your-own-photo stalls seen in bus depots. The interior of the compartment, the control panel of the machine and the floor of the room were spattered with a substance that looked like dried blood.

While I was standing there, the scientist returned and saw me. He was angry, but there wasn't much he could say since my presence was his own fault. He decided to explain everything, on the condition that I agree to keep it off the record. I put my pencil in my pocket.

The apparatus in the corner was a Time machine, he said. The principle of the Time machine, which has obsessed generations of science-fiction writers, actually is rather simple. Many scientists have stumbled across it in recent years, but no public announcement has ever been made.

I asked him why the discoveries had been kept secret.

"Most responsible scientists want nothing to do with a Time machine. They realize no good can come of it. A few investigators have experimented with it, but the results have been so disastrous none of the findings could be published."

"You mean the Time machines don't always work?"

"On the contrary, they work all too well."

My host cited an example. A French physicist, having built himself a Time machine, began by going back to 1812 to dissuade Napoleon from invading Russia. The Frenchman succeeded, incredible as it seems, in actually achieving an interview with the Emperor, which was automatically tape-recorded by the Time machine. After the French scientist finished telling Napoleon about the Russian winter and all that, there was a pause, then two sentences in a crisp military voice. "This man is a traitor. Take him out and shoot him." (Translation.)

The Time machine we were standing in front of had been built, against all advice, by a colleague of my scientist-friend. The builder, a Dr. Potter, had persuaded himself he would conduct research in the remote past and absolutely not meddle in historical matters. Unfortunately, on his first attempt to solve the mystery of the Bering Strait land bridge he ran smack into a sabre-tooth tiger.

"Ugly devil he was, too. He was so close that when we brought Potter back the tiger came along. We had a terrific struggle getting the tiger back into the compartment so we could project him back where he belongs. That's what did all the damage you see here in the lab. Potter was scratched up. Thirteen stitches in his backside, but nothing serious. He was lucky."

Someday I may write the complete history of Time machines. The scientist told me many other fascinating stories that day. Later, I was introduced to Potter and witnessed many of his experiments, some of which involved scholars from other fields.

I honestly think one history professor working with Dr. Potter might have loused up the American Revolution. He had several important members of the Continental Congress excited about a plan to defeat the British at sea with a fleet of steamboats, but when he had craftsmen build a working model he forgot to tell them about safety valves and the model exploded. General Washington was going to hang him as a British saboteur till we switched on the Time machine and rescued him.

An electrical engineer who took a Time trip didn't do any better. He was anxious to improve the lot of the common people during the Middle Ages with a rural electrification project. He was just getting started at a place called Agincourt when he noticed troops of knights and soldiers maneuvering nearby. He associated the name "Agincourt" with a battle, but he seemed to recall that the French had won it. Since he was behind the French lines, he kept right on stringing wire. This error cost him a nasty lump on the side of the head from the handle of an English pikestaff.

I concluded that Time exploration requires broadly educated personnel. All the expeditions so far have had to rely on men who were humanities-oriented and too abstract or technical and too narrow.

I myself have made a couple of short trips in the Time machine. Potter talked me into accompanying him on a journey to study the advance of glaciers in North America. I made him go first to make sure there were no sabre-tooths or mammoths hanging around. When I got there—somewhere in Minnesota about 200,000 B.C.—it was snowing so hard I couldn't see a thing. I stamped around in the snow looking for Potter until my feet hurt from the cold. I couldn't find him so I returned to the twentieth century and shared a hot toddy with the lab assistant. By the time Potter came back he had frostbitten ears.

Another time—July 29, 1588, to be exact—I happened to be in Plymouth, England, when some sailors rushed up to me and cried, "The Armada is coming." I didn't say a word. I know how to keep out of trouble. However, I did stroll over to the bowling green to watch Sir Francis Drake finish his game. He lost.

I would have traveled more extensively in Time had not Potter's experiments ended abruptly. On one of his solo journeys Potter visited a prehistoric cannibal tribe about to sacrifice a young maiden. He tried to talk them out of it and succeeded rather better than he expected.

They ate him instead.

After that, the other scientists at the Institute were too disheartened to continue the Time machine experiments. Some of the young research assistants rebuilt Potter's machine into a computer that has distinguished itself by picking the daily double at Arlington Park twenty-three times.

The Last Train Out of Foolihow

When Caslon "Chip" Bodoni was a young reporter, none of the other staffers would have believed that someday he would be perhaps the best-known journalist in the country. Nothing about him suggested that much fame and success in his future. How-

ever, in later years they recalled they hadn't had the opportunity
to know him well.

Chip worked from four o'clock to midnight, which is the
skeleton shift on an afternoon paper. After about six o'clock
there was no one in the office but Chip and the other skele-
tons—a desk man, a rewrite man, a photographer and a copyboy.
Since there was no deadline during this shift, Chip had plenty
of time to try to slake the burning curiosity of the editors who
worked days thinking up investigative assignments for him.

He frequently found himself scooting nervously along dark
alleys and tenement hallways in parts of the city where policemen went only in pairs. He began carrying a flashlight in his
topcoat pocket, partly because it helped him avoid falling down
rat holes in the dark and partly because he considered it a useful
weapon. It was a long flashlight with a heavy metal case, with
which he felt he had a chance of standing off muggers if there
weren't more than seven or eight of them.

Bodoni didn't enjoy these expeditions. He was not the kind
of reporter eager to maintain reader interest in his paper by
slipping down a chimney with a stethoscope to eavesdrop on
the Mafia at risk of being put into a concrete bathing suit. The
one reader whose interests truly mattered to him was himself.

One day a gang of young hoodlums bungled a bank robbery.
The youngest contrived to lock himself in the vault and couldn't
get away with the others. Resentful, he gave the police and the
press the names and addresses of his accomplices. A few
hours later, with the rest of the gang in jail, Bodoni was ordered
to visit their homes and try to pick up a second-day story.

"Talk to their mothers and the neighbors. Find out if they
were always bad boys," the desk man directed.

Chip took a bus as close as he could to the first address. The
sun was setting as he walked west along a quiet street of small
houses forty or fifty years old. Watching the house numbers as
he walked, he realized that the address he was looking for had
to be a couple of blocks farther on. But as he reached the end
of the block he came to the end of the houses. Stretching ahead

of him was one of the large tracts of open land that still remain in the midst of cities because the land is swampy or zoned for buggy-whip factories or held off the market by speculators. Near the middle of the tract stood a single house, a dilapidated frame building covered with tar paper false brick and surrounded by odds and ends of junk: an auto lacking wheels and engine, an old sink, empty packing cases. Parked around the front steps were three or four motorcycles.

That was the house, ominous-looking, not the kind of place where you'd be deferentially received by the butler.

Chip stood at the corner and imagined the scene he might expect. Knock, knock. The door opens. Three or four tough-looking punks are inside. One says, "Yeah?"

"I'm Caslon Bodoni from the *Gazette*. Is this where Peanuts Glutz lives?"

"Yeah. Waddabout it?"

"What was he like before he was arrested this afternoon for bank robbery? Was he ever in trouble before?"

"Youse are goddam nosy, ain't you? Peanuts is my brudder, and I hate nosy bastards asking a lot of goddam questions about my brudder. Let's get him, guys."

Bodoni considered the isolated position of the house and estimated the probability of anyone hearing cries for help at zero. He dialed another channel of his imagination and tried again. This time the door was answered by Ma Glutz, a dumpy slattern in a filthy housedress who threatened to cut out his heart with her paring knife.

Bodoni didn't like that program any better, so he turned and walked back to the bus stop, where there was a drug store with a pay telephone.

"Give me the city desk. . . . Pete? . . . This is Bodoni. . . . Yes, I went to the Glutz house. Nobody home. No neighbors, either. The house sits by itself out in the middle of a big open field. No story here. . . . Shouldn't I take a break for dinner now?"

The editors could never catch Chip shirking, but they sensed he was not likely to risk his neck. When the day came that they needed a man to send overseas on a dangerous assignment, he ordinarily would not have been considered. A more logical choice would have been "Iron Hat" Hansen, who hadn't taken his hat off even to sleep since he first saw *The Front Page* and had sent fourteen politicians to jail. Or Flash Fogarty, who got to the scene before the police so often that seven of the paper's press cars had been shot from under him. Or, for that matter, any of several other members of the staff distinguished for fleetness of foot when chased by a mob or coolness when the police started shooting off their guns. But this one had heavy family responsibilities, that one's health wasn't what it used to be. For one reason or another, no one was available to go on short notice but Chip.

His boss called him into the private office used only for hiring and firing. "Bodoni, fighting has just broken out in South Chaos. We've decided to send a correspondent. Here's your plane ticket and some expense money. Get over there and find out what's going on."

A few days later Bodoni had filed his first story from his comfortable room at the Chaos Hilton. He couldn't say he knew what was going on. However, by diligent inquiry he had located the South Chaotian Ministry of Information and had begun to cultivate rapport with the chief press officer.

Chip knew that even in covering a minor riot a reporter is to some extent at the mercy of the authorities. He can see for himself what is happening in front of his eyes, but part of the story always involves what happened before he arrived at the scene, what is happening simultaneously in several other places, and what the response of the authorities is going to be in the future. Since the authorities are rarely if ever completely candid, the art of reporting involves not only writing a vivid and accurate account of what the reporter sees for himself but also sifting out gleaming little nuggets of probable truth from everything other people tell him.

The chief press officer was more helpful than most. He spoke

English poorly and none of the press corps understood much Chaotian. Consequently, the correspondents were only slightly misled by the government's official lies.

Chip's best news source, as usual, was another reporter, Sam Serif, whose paper had sent him to Chaos several weeks earlier. Sam knew his way around. When they struck up an acquaintance in the hotel bar, Sam filled him in on the art of war correspondence as well as on the general situation in Chaos.

"When you cover a war, Chip, it's dangerous to go any place anything important might happen where you can see it. They're shooting real bullets. On the other hand, the boss used to be a reporter himself. He already suspects you of working out of the hotel bar by rewriting the local papers and government press handouts. And it's hard to sound authentic day in and day out when you're working with third- and fourth-hand sources.

"What I do is go out from time to time to where there are some American troops and talk to them. Nothing convinces your editor that you are working better than a story liberally sprinkled with names and quotations from actual soldiers. You can make up the quotations, but the names have to be real. If you can't find a soldier from your paper's metropolitan marketing area, look for the nineteen-year-old corporal from Iowa. Every outfit has one and he counts almost as many points as a local boy."

Chip paid for the drinks and ordered another round. Sam explained the background of the current war. East Chaos and West Chaos had been fighting off and on for years, mostly border skirmishes. The fighting had been restrained by the fact that the only good east-west pass through the mountains lay in South Chaotian territory. At the intersection of this pass with the only good north-south pass was the city of Foolihow, one hundred miles north of their Chaos Hilton base. The North Chaotians, who favored the East Chaotians and harbored ancient grudges against the South Chaotians, had recently invaded South Chaos. The North Chaotians apparently intended to seize Foolihow with its two strategic passes and unleash the

East Chaotians against the West Chaotians. The East Chaotians had been holding back because they didn't wish to antagonize South Chaos and because of a superstitious reverence for an old Chaotian proverb:

"Man who not realize east-west pass run both ways may have to do some running himself."

Sam concluded: "Much as I hate to stick my neck out I'm afraid I'll have to go to Foolihow so I can at least get the right dateline on my cables."

Chip paled. "I won't go to Foolihow and risk getting killed even if they threaten to fire me."

Three days later Chip went to Foolihow to risk getting killed. They had threatened to fire him if he didn't.

Chip and Sam found the situation in Foolihow more desperate than they had anticipated. No Foolihow Hilton. No hotel bar. No Ministry of Information. No translators to help them plagiarize the local paper. No one seemed able to tell them what was happening, although they could hear artillery fire up the pass to the north and suspected the North Chaotian army might be getting closer.

The nearest American troops were far to the south. Washington hadn't yet decided whose side they were on. It was hard to tell which side were the Communists. The conflict seemed to be shaping up North and East against South and West. The South was OK, except for a quirk about states' rights, and the North looked quite red to the State Department. But our potential allies, the West Chaotians, were much farther left than the North and the East wasn't red at all. The State Department couldn't even put its chips on the underdog yet because as near as anyone could tell the whole pack of Chaotians were underdogs and had been underdogs for centuries.

Sam Serif finally managed to find the headquarters of the defending general, which was disguised as a gasoline station. (When the war was dull, the general augmented his income by greasing trucks.) The general had a staff officer who more or less spoke English and was in charge of press relations and tire and battery sales.

For several days this officer furnished Chip and Sam with news. Becoming friendly, he offered them a jeep and an armed escort to the front line north of Foolihow, where they could watch the progress of the battle first-hand.

"You ought to go, Chip," Sam said. "You have a duty to the readers of your newspaper to keep them fully informed of the progress of world affairs so they can participate in the democratic process on the basis of complete information."

"You must be kidding. The enemy won't know I'm a peaceful agent of the democratic process. They might shoot me. Or, more likely, our friends the South Chaotians will get me. You know what bad shots they are. Besides, I know my paper's readers. They're a lip-moving lot who never get past the funnies."

While Chip and Sam were talking, the press officer was taking a telephone call. When he hung up, he warned that to the consternation of defense headquarters the North Chaotians had broken through and seemed likely to encircle the city within twenty-four hours. The last train was going to leave the depot in half an hour.

"I have a hunch," Sam said, "that the next big story is going to break in the bar at the Chaos Hilton." He ran out the door— several paces behind Bodoni, who was already headed for the depot at top speed.

This was the moment of crisis in which Bodoni's talent for self-preservation was to find full expression. At the depot, a huge throng was already pushing and shoving to get aboard the last train, which obviously could not carry all who wished to ride. All Bodoni and Serif could see were the backs of the people surrounding the train. Bodoni reached into the pocket of his trench coat and pulled out his flashlight. He stepped up to the nearest Chaotian and rapped him on the head. Then the next. Crack! Crack! Crack! As scores crumpled to the ground, the alarmed survivors edged away from the maniac with the flashlight just enough to open a narrow lane to the train.

Chip pushed ahead quickly to the front row, where he saw the last obstacle—a ring of soldiers saving space on the last car for the general's truck tools. With fixed bayonets they were holding the crowd back. Chip raised his flashlight above his head. The metal case glittered in the intense Chaotian sunlight.

"You-fella walkee walkee chop chop," he shouted above the noise of the crowd in an attempt at pidgin English, which he hoped the soldiers might remember from British colonial days. "Him-fella new kind Amelican handgrenade full of napalm. Walkee walkee or I'll burn your bloomin' arses to a crisp."

Trying to save face (as well as other expanses of anatomy), the soldiers looked away as Chip dragged Sam with him into the coach just as the train began to move. Sam had been accidentally conked on the head and knocked out by the flailing flashlight at the height of the excitement. Since he remained unconscious the rest of the day and was unable to work for two or three days thereafter, only one man—Caslon Bodoni—could give the waiting world an eye-witness account of the fall of Foolihow. As is well known, this was the beginning of Bodoni's rise to prominence.

Long May It Wave
o'er the Land of the Careful

My friend Bunker, who long has been suffering from coffee nerves, dandruff and a neurotic fear of crabgrass, has something new to worry about. He thinks the government is planning to shoot him.

He is upset by the talk in Washington favoring a strict Federal law against desecrating the flag. Congressman James H. Quillen of Tennessee wants to haul flag desecrators before

a firing squad and shoot them. Congressman Mason O'Neal of
Georgia would hold a sedition trial for anyone who abuses the
flag orally. Poor Bunker has been desecrating the flag for years,
and he's sure they're after him.

He doesn't mean to desecrate the flag. It's not that he's trying
to dissent from the Federal Migratory Bird Act or anything. His
trouble is that he lives on a patriotic block and he's afraid not to
display the flag in front of his house from sunrise to sunset on
New Year's Day, Inauguration Day, Lincoln's Birthday, Washington's Birthday, Armed Forces Day, Easter Sunday, Mother's
Day, Memorial Day, Flag Day, Independence Day, Labor Day,
Constitution Day, Columbus Day, Armistice Day, Thanksgiving
Day, Christmas Day and such other days as may be proclaimed
by the President of the United States. The neighbors might
think he was getting soft on Communism if they didn't see his
flag out there with the rest.

As a result of flying the flag, he commits several offenses
every holiday. He never hoists the flag till long after sunrise and
has been known to forget to take it down at sunset. One Fourth
of July there was a sudden thundershower that drenched the
flag. Wet and heavy, it drooped down into the daisies—another
offense.

Bunker is still more criminal when he takes his children to the
Fourth-of-July parade. There are always vendors selling small
flags on sticks. He tries to hold out every year, but the children
cry and threaten to lie down in the street in front of a self-
propelled missile launcher so he has no choice but to buy the
flags for them. Then the flag desecration begins. The children,
who are small, quickly weary of holding the sticks upright. Their
arms sag lower and lower until the flags are dragging on the
ground. If Bunker isn't alert every second, the children may
even drop the flags in front of him and he may walk on them
without noticing until he feels the stick crunching underfoot.

When Bunker and the little Hills go home from the parade,
he is likely to lose track of the flags, assuming they have been
lost along the way. The next thing he knows the dog is sleeping

on one. Or the baby has taken the cloth off the stick and wrapped it around a doll. Bunker tries to avoid such shocking instances of flag desecration by picking up the little flags and burning them as soon as the children go to bed.

"But suppose I'm caught burning the flags sometime," he said to me. "Nobody will believe I'm only disposing of the flag in a dignified way, preferably by burning, when it is in such condition that it is no longer a fitting emblem for display."

"I can see you have memorized the flag display rules," I said. "Don't you realize those congressmen aren't after patriotic citizens like yourself? They only want to do something about people who burn flags because they disagree with the government's policies."

"Don't think I disagree with the government's policies," Bunker quickly replied, with beads of sweat appearing on his brow. "But what if I disagree with a government policy accidentally? One I never heard of and don't know anything about? There I am late at night out by the leaf burner. This little kid's flag has chocolate ice cream dribbled all over it and I am patriotically burning it. An FBI agent steps out of the bushes and says, 'Good evening, Mr. Hill, I was just passing by when I happened to wonder whether you think Monaco should sign a trade agreement with Albania.' I say it's OK with me, then it turns out our State Department is against it. I'm caught red-white-and-blue-handed—a flag-burning dissenter!"

"You exaggerate, Bunker," I told him. "It probably will only count if you commit the offense in public. You'd have to announce in advance you were burning the flag not because it was in such condition that it was no longer a fitting emblem for display but because you wished to express your disagreement with whatever the government was doing that bothered you."

Bunker looked relieved. "You mean they wouldn't get me because when I watch the late movie on television I don't wait for them to finish playing 'The Star-Spangled Banner' at the end but just go to sleep?"

I had to admit I couldn't guess what the congressional firing squad had in mind. However, I pointed out to Bunker that everyone knew him to be a citizen who always sunburned his bald spot at the Fourth of July parade taking off his hat for every flag that went by no matter how many there were. I told him that should count heavily in his favor if he ever did find himself picked up on a flag desecration charge.

After soothing Bunker, I began to wonder myself about certain other cases. What if the altar boy in some parish put the flag on the wrong side of the altar some Sunday morning? Shooting him would raise the constitutional issues of freedom of religion and separation of church and state.

And what about politicians who make flag-waving speeches? This is a time-honored political technique for taking the voters' minds off the real issues. The courts might interpret a tough Federal flag-protection statute as a ban on figurative flag waving. Then a lot of politicians would be in trouble. They might have to confront their constituents with reason and facts instead of patriotic emotions.

I was a bit nervous about my own case for a while. We have an electric train engine with two little flags that fit into sockets at the front. They're less than half an inch long, but they have the right number of stripes and, I think, stars. Despite my firm policy with juvenile flag desecrators (we use the rack, moderately), these flags frequently can be found laying on my basement floor in a disrespectful manner. If the Feds ever raided the place, I'd be in trouble myself.

But when I read in the papers that several of the most vehement supporters of a Federal anti-desecration law are congressmen from the South, I felt more comfortable. I realized they probably are talking about forbidding desecration of the *Confederate* flag, and I don't have a single one of those on the premises.

That's the Way the Martyr's Head Bounces

When you get to a certain age, you suddenly discover you have
a remarkable memory for the plots of prehistoric movies. The
other day I happened to think about one film in which a non-
chalant bum symbolized the intellectual in relation to current
affairs.

In the movie, the advisers of a fictional candidate for the
Presidency found out that a certain precinct had always voted
for the winner in every election on record. This fact suggested
a publicity campaign to start the bandwagon rolling for their
man. Adding interest was the circumstance that in the bell-
wether precinct at the time lived only one registered voter—a
bum with no visible means of support.

The publicity campaign made a national figure of him as
he appeared in countless photographs at the side of the candidate. He was maintained in luxury throughout the campaign at
the candidate's expense.

Told on election night that the candidate had won, the bum
remarked, in one of Hollywood's greatest punch lines: "He's not
a bad sort. I almost wish I had voted for him myself."

Aloof, uninvolved, ungrateful, perfectly willing to bite the
hand that fed him, the bum was much like the intellectuals
who pass judgment on contemporary affairs.

Some observers have registered shock at the critical bent of
intellectuals, saying they never before have been treated so well.
Artists and writers used to starve in garrets; now they latch onto
fellowships or become "poets in residence" at universities.
College and university professors, after the lean years, have been
receiving one salary increase after another. Scientists can easily
lay hands on a couple of million dollars for new laboratories and

equipment whenever they want. Musicians and actors, with a few residuals coming in from television commercials, can afford to spend three quarters of their time loafing or dabbling in experimental theater as they choose. Journalists, clergymen and assorted other eggheads have secretaries and credit cards. Unlike ordinary folks, intellectuals don't punch time clocks, and when they travel, it's always at someone else's expense.

And how does the intellectual repay society for his comfortable living, his airconditioned studio, his expense account from the Foundation and numerous perquisites of prestige?

He complains.

There he sits in his walnut-paneled study, beaming genially over a glass of good scotch. Perhaps he's ripping up the economic system. What's so good, he asks, about a system that denies its benefits to certain classes, such as migratory farm workers, Indians, uneducated Negroes, residents of depressed areas, the aged poor and other groups? Someone requests his opinion of Communism. He doesn't think much of that either, since Communists make economic decisions for political reasons and vice versa with results that often are disastrous for their own people.

And that's not all. Big business, big labor and big government are strangling the economy, such as it is. Better they should strangle each other. He's in favor of building a new system, which he says is evolving anyhow.

He refills his glass with scotch and turns to another subject. Religion? The message is revolutionary but the institutions are reactionary—probably the most conservative force in the world. The Catholics are in turmoil, he says, because the revolt against the monarchical principle which occurred in the political world a century or more ago is finally, after the usual cultural lag, getting around to undermining the Church's discipline. The Protestants are flustered because even the names of their denominations keep changing. When someone points out the value of recent reforms, he snorts and says they don't go far enough.

Politics? Foreign affairs? Customs and manners? He views

them all with alarm. He finds reason to complain even about the prosperity of the fine arts. The ordinary man is showing unprecedented interest in the arts, thronging museums and concerts, and spending his money to support artistic enterprises on a lavish scale. Alas, mourns the intellectual, the arts are being vulgarized. It may have been better when artists had aristocratic patrons. (Of course, one of Bach's royal patrons once threw him into jail, but one has to admire the Duke's aristocratic standards.)

No matter what subject is mentioned the intellectual can find fault with the *status quo*. He is a viper in the bosom of society.

By temperament, he's a non-conformist. If he wanted to follow the herd, he never would have chosen architecture or biochemical research or poetry as his life's work. By training, he is a critic. Art and science can advance only through constant reappraisal of the work that has already been done.

But society doesn't much like non-conformity and searching criticism. The intellectual is always under pressure to keep his opinions to himself, and there are plenty of soft-boiled eggheads who do in fact give up the struggle.

One type gives up entirely and moves to a pad in a beatnik neighborhood. The dropouts may continue to criticize the state of affairs, but they do it from outside, without much of an audience. Some of this criticism is, however, valuable because of its unusual purity.

Other intellectuals sell out. They are the scholars who kowtow to those university administrations more interested in raising funds than standards. They are the experts who can be depended upon to testify in behalf of the *status quo* at legislative hearings. They are the artists who put their talent to commercial use exclusively.

Fortunately, there are intellectuals who neither reject society entirely nor cuddle up all the way. There's nothing ignoble about tolerating society and its institutions up to a point. It is part of man's better nature to avoid being a burden to his aging parents, to support a family, to do the job he is paid to do for the sake of clients, fellow employees, stockholders, students or other dependents, including the tax-needy government.

A reasonable man, even if he happens to be an intellectual, can't complain all the time, about everything. Occasionally, public affairs are in such good order that for the time being a critic has nothing much to say. Also, he needs some of his time and energy to work at whatever branch of knowledge or art supports his claim to be an intellectual.

The test of an intellectual's integrity is whether he ever stops complaining altogether. If he seldom or never finds anything to view with alarm, he was never a genuine intellectual in the first place, despite his occupation, or else he has traded in his Phi Beta Kappa key for stock in the Mess o' Pottage Cereal Company.

Americans are uncomfortable with abstract words like "intellectual." I never heard of anyone who would stand with his elbow on the bar and say, "Me? I'm an intellectual." No one identifies himself as a scientist or an artist either. A man will say, "I'm a biologist" or "I write books" or "I teach history." Nevertheless, there is a class of persons who recognize themselves and each other as intellectuals and agree to observe the rules. Rule 1: the intellectual must persevere in his questioning and complaining even when it becomes dangerous. Obeying this rule is the just price of his perquisites.

Intellectuals are the prophets of today. Many are false prophets, to be sure, but their works of art, the direction of their research, their writings and speeches—all seek the truth. If this means loss of a job, trouble getting a passport or an uncomfortable session with a hostile congressional committee instead of selection by the Book-of-the-Month Club or a professorship at Harvard, that's the way the martyr's head bounces. Martyrdom has always been part of the prophet's vocation.

When the intellectuals stop complaining, it is either because a culture has died and there aren't any intellectuals left or because a police state has locked them all up. In a healthy society, all that diverts them from complaining about affairs generally is the pleasure of complaining about each other.

Like any concerned citizen, I sometimes worry about the health of our society. Then I turn to the books and journals through which the intellectuals make their voices heard. They are saying conditions are appalling in numerous departments of our national life, that stupidity and rascality are exceeded only by the prevalence of paranoia. I am greatly cheered. As long as everything's all wrong, all's right with the world, and the commonwealth rests secure.